Iron Nekkid
and
You'll Always
Get Burned

• • • • • • • • • • • • • • • • • •

Iron Nekkid and You'll Always Get Burned

· ·

Bob Morris

with a Middleword by
Dave Barry

SENTINEL BOOKS

An imprint of Tribune Books
Sentinel Communications Company
Orlando / 1992

Edited by Stephen R. Vaughn
Designed by Eileen M. Schechner
Cover photograph by Tom Spitz
Back cover photograph of
Queen Kumquat Sashay parade by Phelan M. Ebenhack

Printed in the United States by R.R. Donnelley

ISBN 0-941263-39-8

For R.J. and Georgiana,
who still claim me
as their own.

More than just an introduction!

I'm still not sure how we came up with the title for this book. As the author I was hoping for something different. Something powerful, yet simple. But my attorney warned there might be problems if we called it *Schwarzenegger!*

Then one of the editors of this book said: "You know what column of yours I really liked? I really liked that column you wrote about ironing nekkid."

For the record, this editor's name is Dixie Kasper.[1] I think she should be held as responsible for the title of this book as I am.

I wasn't really surprised that out of all the newspaper columns I have ever written[2] that Dixie Kasper would most fondly remember the one she did. It proves my Dark Suit Theory of column writing.

You see, every now and then[3] I will sit down and attempt to write a column on one of the Important Issues of Our Times. I will conduct interviews with Noted Authorities. I will gather bushel baskets full of Raw Facts. Then I will distill all my Lofty Thoughts and Salient Opinions into a column so profound, so penetrating, so right-on-target that it will surely rectify man's inhumanity to man, achieve lasting world peace and restore the price of premium beer to less than $3 a six-pack. This splendid column will appear in the paper. I will smugly await the applause, the acclaim, the inevitable Pulitzer nomination. And . . . and writing one of those columns, I've found, is a lot like wetting your pants while you're wearing a dark suit. You get a nice, warm feeling. And no one notices.

(1) When your name is Dixie you just naturally say "nekkid" even though alleged proper English maintains you should say "naked" or "in the nude." But then, the rules of proper English are half-bekkid.
(2) The last time I tried to count them the number was closing in on 2,500. At an average of 900 words per column that is approximately 2,250,000, which is 100 times as many words as Ernest Hemingway put in *The Old Man and the Sea,* which won him the Nobel Prize and which is the sort of math writers often perform to encourage themselves to drink more hard liquor.
(3) Usually after having watched too much public television.

Instead, what people notice is when you write a perfectly stupid column about ironing nekkid — like this one:

I have my reasons for ironing nekkid. For one thing, my wife will not iron for me. I don't expect her to. The ability to iron with finesse a 100 percent cotton shirt is the mark of a gentleman — a gentleman who cannot afford dry cleaning.

Still, ironing is a highly-refined skill and one that can give me something to fall back on should the column writing business bottom out. I could always find work as some gentleman's valet. Assuming the gentleman was open-minded about nekkid valets.

Another reason I iron nekkid is because I am a heavy sweater. No, hell no. Not a cable knit. Not a lambswool crew neck from L.L. Bean. I misstated myself, all right? What I meant to say was: I sweat heavily.

Heavy sweating is a function of living in Florida. Heavy sweating is good for you. People who live in Florida and try to avoid heavy sweating always wind up miserable. Mainly because, in their futile attempt to make the subtropics temperate, they must assign 40 percent of their disposable income directly to Florida Power & Light.

Before I took up nekkid ironing I would sweat heavily while I ironed. When I put on my freshly-ironed clothes, the sweat would blotch them and I would become The Incredible Wrinkled Man. Not that I have a reputation for fastidiousness or anything. It's just that I hate to see my ironing so instantly undone.

Iron nekkid and you plug in free to God's own AC. Iron nekkid and you slip into your clothes refreshed, ready to face the world wrinkle-free and without wet pits. Iron nekkid and you feel like you are really getting away with something.

Another thing: A nekkid ironer is a careful ironer. For obvious reasons. Concentration is the nekkid ironer's most important ally. Sure, I've been scorched a time or two in strategic places. Iron nekkid and you'll always get burned. Eventually. But that's a small price to pay for collars without unsightly creases. Don't you think?

Besides, ironing nekkid is wonderfully efficient. Especially for those of us who are not capable of planning ahead. I am not one of those people who, when stepping into a shower, already has his clothes spread out on the bed, ready to put on. I don't even have them picked out. Not only that, but when I finally get around to showering it's usually at the absolute last minute, just before I'm supposed to be somewhere.

So when I'm hurrying to iron my clothes, you can't actually

expect me to waste precious seconds putting on other clothes that will only be worn for a couple of lousy minutes, can you? Ironing nekkid is abundantly justified. Ironing nekkid would be recommended by the best-selling authors of time management books if only they had the courage to try it.

My wife is unimpressed by all the time I save ironing nekkid.

"If you are saving all that time then how come the back porch soffit still needs fixing?" she demands. "If you ask me, the way you iron is just another one of your dumb quirks."

I don't know if it's a quirk that will be passed on to my sons. They seem to be developing dumb quirks of their own, like their strange fascination with garage door openers.

See, one of them takes the remote control opener from my car. The other one grabs the bottom of the garage door. Then the first one punches the remote control while the other one, laughing all the way, gets a free ride, then drops down just before he gets mangled. Yes, I've warned them about the dangers. And I've had to repair the garage door twice. Still, they are boys and this is how they get their jollies.

Oh, did I mention that we keep our ironing board in the garage? That's where I iron nekkid.

And that's where I was that fateful day, putting the finishing touches on a blue oxford, when I heard the clinkety-clank-clinking of the garage door. Through the quickly widening crack I saw one son outside with the remote control and the other son in midair, shrieking with delight.

I am a conscientious father. I want to mold my children into responsible adults. And I will gladly drop everything I am doing to help them along their way, even at the expense of my own well-being.

So, yes, I temporarily forgot just how vulnerable I was while I delivered yet another fatherly lecture on the hazards of riding the garage door. A helpful hint to parents: Kids tend to pay amazingly close attention when they get surprise lectures from nekkid fathers.

Oh . . . and did I mention that there's this nice, little lady from down the street who likes to walk her dog by our house each day? Did I mention that this nice, little lady chose that precise instant to make her rounds?

Ma'am, I know it was ungentlemanly of me to rush off the way I did without so much as a hello, clutching my blue oxford around me and wrinkling it all to hell.

I do hope you'll walk by again someday. I'd like the chance to explain myself. I'd like the chance to tell you about one of my dumb quirks.

CAUTION: INCOMING METAPHOR!

It occurred to me, while rereading that piece, that writing a newspaper column is a lot like ironing nekkid.

At least, I'm willing to make that connection as I struggle to rationalize why we called this book what we called it and why we put me nekkid on the cover to illustrate it.[4]

I have my reasons for writing a newspaper column. For one thing, my wife will not write it for me. And while I don't presume for an instant that the ability to write a newspaper column is the mark of a gentleman, nothing else I am capable of doing would rank high in refinement either.

I am not the sort of columnist who plans ahead. All the columns in this book were written at the absolute last minute.[5] It's not like I have a closetful of freshly-pressed columns that I can just slip into the paper.

I start out each morning with an idea that is not at all presentable, something often yanked straight out of the dirty clothes hamper that is daydreaming. Then I warm up my word processor and try to get rid of all the wrinkles.

On rare days I luck into one of those remarkable Permanent Press ideas and all I have to do is touch it up a little. Mostly though, I plod along, trying to steam out dead-end pockets of digression and put a sharp crease in the sleeve of opinion. Just when I think I've got the fabric looking sharp I flip it over to find I've botched up the collar of credibility.

If only there were a spray starch for words, a One Hour Column Dry Cleaner.

I am a slow, slow writer.[6] I sweat heavy over each and every column. This has not prompted me to take up nekkid column writing. Yet.

But then writing a column automatically leaves you exposed. There is no nekkidness like the nekkidness that comes from baring your thoughts (and your ignorance) four days a week in the newspaper.

Most readers are kind and forgiving when I occasionally show my butt. And they do the sensible thing – they ignore me.

Others are more than happy to let me know they've caught me

(4) Pity Tom Spitz, the photographer, and Joe Gosen, the guy who kept fiddling with the lighting. The two of them were forced to share the studio with nekkid me for the two photo sessions and six hours it took to finally come up with the cover shot. Spitz and Gosen are amazing photo technicians. I especially admire how they made it look like I am 30 pounds heavier than I really am.

(5) Now seems as good a time as any to acknowledge those *Orlando Sentinel* editors who have patiently dealt with my column on a daily basis: Sal Recchi, Mike Bales, Jay Hamburg, Joyce Jones, Barry Glenn, David Burch, Susan Whigham, Wendy Spirduso and Mark Skoneki. Thanks for your kind cuts and gentle proddings. But please understand it gives me great pleasure to relegate you to a footnote.

(6) I am two weeks late with this introduction and receiving semi-violent computer messages from Dixie even as I write this.

with my pants down. But that comes with the turf.

Write a newspaper column and you'll always get burned.

I'll let you in on a secret: There are lots of mornings when I sit down to read the newspaper and I simply cannot stand to even look at my column. It can be a perfectly good column, a column with no major fact errors, fairly acceptable grammar, nothing that's criminally libelous and yet I can't bring myself to glance at it. I turn my eyes because the words I've put down there are just too revealing. I'm embarrassed. I have to cover up the side of the paper that contains my column.

Much like I tried to cover up myself when that nice, little lady from down the street walked by with her dog.

For those of you who've strolled into this book . . . welcome. Especially those of you who first read these columns in the newspaper and shelled out more money so you could read them again.[7]

I don't mean to be ungentlemanly. I hate to rush off. But, please, excuse me. The garage door is going up. And I'm running for cover.

(7) Thanks to George Biggers, Steve Vaughn, Eileen Schechner and Ken Paskman for performing the sleight-of-hand necessary to turn an unsightly heap o' columns into a fairly presentable book. Still, I trust all of you will buy multiple copies.

Guys Without Women

THE WONDERFUL THING ABOUT being married to the woman I am married to is that she understands, explicitly, how we guys need to get together on a regular basis to carouse and howl at the moon and do all the dumb, predictable, endearing things guys do when we get together away from the women we are married to.

"I am thinking about going out of town with the guys next weekend," I tell my wife.

"I am thinking about buying a new dining room table," she says.

"We will probably be gone two nights," I say.

"I will probably get six chairs to go with the table," she says.

"I figure we're going to do a little fishing, play some poker, that sort of thing."

"I figure the table and the chairs are going to cost around $3,700."

It's all a matter of communication. I feel very strongly that most marital difficulties could be easily avoided if more men and women were willing to occasionally sit down and talk honestly like this.

At the risk of betraying my gender, I would like to share a secret with you women. I know that some of you are suspicious of your menfolk when they say they are going off on weekend trips with the guys. You suspect they might, just might, be going off to fool around.

Here is how you can tell what they are really up to: Pay close attention to how much stuff they take with them.

If your man packs lightly, but actually remembers to take his toothbrush, then it is probably time to pop for the private detective.

If, however, he goes through endless fits of agony trying to find all the stuff he wants to take and keeps cussing about how, dammit, it is time to buy a full-sized pickup, then you can be assured of his fidelity. Especially if, once he's down the road, you notice that he's left his toothbrush.

Now, I realize that I am backing myself into a politically incorrect corner here by insinuating that "stuff" is a replacement for women.

Please understand, I don't endorse this state of affairs. But I do accept it. I fear it is biologically inescapable. And I am merely trying to explain the way it works.

For instance, on this particular weekend trip, I was packed when the guys arrived. And still we spent another hour making sure we didn't leave important stuff behind.

"What about a Rand McNally road atlas?" I'd say.

"We've already got two," one of the guys would say.

"But better bring it anyway," the other ones would urge.

"What about my new propane lantern?" I'd ask.

"Well, we've already got seven flashlights and a kerosene lantern . . . "

"But better bring it anyway."

"What about some WD-40?"

"Can't ever have too much WD-40 . . . "

And so it went. There were four of us. We were to be gone for roughly 48 hours. And we were taking a boat, spinning tackle, fly-fishing tackle, deep-sea tackle, six tackle boxes, God knows how many ice coolers, a cast net, three sailboards, snorkeling gear, three Yucatan hammocks, five pairs of binoculars, tennis rackets, racquetball rackets, one of those beach paddleball games, three decks of playing cards, three boom boxes, each of our complete collections of cassette tapes, two horseshoe sets and you don't want to know how much beer.

It wasn't nearly enough. Beer, that is.

So what do guys do when they get together away from women? Well, depends.

Guys are much more flexible than women. Having packed all that stuff to take on a trip, women, being the pragmatic species, would actually feel compelled to use it.

Not guys. For guys, just having all that stuff nearby is enough.

Because mostly what guys do is sit around and discuss what it is they should do.

"Could go fishing."

"Could."

"Could go windsurfing."

"Could."

"Could play horseshoes."

"Could."

"Say. Could you reach me another beer?"

There are two things that guys always do on guy trips: play poker and discuss who among them is responsible for the most offensive bodily odors.

Women, I don't know how to tell you this, but guys will spend a great deal more time discussing noxious odors than they will discussing women. It's unforgivable. I know. But it's just the way it is.

Occasionally, there will be a call to action.

"What do you suppose might happen," asked one of the guys on our trip, "if you fed Alka-Seltzer to one of those sea gulls that keeps pestering us?"

Guys will ponder a question like this for a long time. They will turn it over and over, in and out. Bets might well be placed. And then they will pile into the car and drive 20 miles round trip to the nearest convenience store just to buy some Alka-Seltzer. Because out of all that stuff they didn't bring any along.

For the record: You gotta disguise the Alka-Seltzer in a piece of bread to get the sea gull to eat it. Unfortunately, they fly away before they really start to foam.

Before we headed home from our guys trip, we put all our stuff in a big pile and found someone to take our picture with it. I am planning to have my copy framed. And I've got a place picked out where I can look at it every evening. While I sit at our new dining room table.

Building Better Floridians

(CAUTION: THE FOLLOW-ing column contains a frank discussion of evolutionary theory. If there is even the slightest chance that this might prove contrary to your personal beliefs, then we suggest you leave the room immediately).

Whew, now that they're gone we can kick back a little. Because we aren't really going to discuss evolutionary theory. We're just going to blindly accept it as fact.

The only flaw with evolution is that it takes too long to happen. That's why, even as you read this, the Japanese are working on a device that would speed up the evolutionary process. I don't know all the details, but it involves fine-tuning another one of their inventions – the fast-forward function on VCRs.

And, if all goes well, human beings will soon be able to prepare their own evolutionary shopping lists. In preparation for that happy day, let's consider a few much-needed anatomical changes that would benefit all of us living in Florida ...

The DEET Gland: If you've ever read the list of ingredients on a can of "Deep Woods Off" then you obviously have too much time on your hands. But you also know that DEET stands for "N,N-diethyl-meta-touamide" and is the major ingredient in mosquito repellent. Future Floridians, if they choose to evolve, will have a DEET Gland located at the base of their necks. It will automatically secrete potent, death-dealing DEET at the mere buzzing of biting insects or the utterance of such phrases as: "Imagine! This entire subdivision used to be a swamp." Or, "Hey, let's keep on fishing after it gets dark."

The Ray-Ban Sheath: So how many pairs of sunglasses have you lost or destroyed in the past year? You live in Florida, you gotta have shades. I envision a transparent, yet Polarized, eyelid that will eventually form behind the existing eyelid, further protecting the eyeball. It will be a voluntary organ, instantly descending when an individual steps outside or has been overindulging in illegal substances.

Three-Pronged Socket: Here in Florida there is no such thing as too much electricity. So our bodies need at least one handy electrical outlet. Say where our right elbow used to be. We're talking 220 volts of alternating current (a solar battery will first form in the right armpit). Good place to plug in one of those nifty portable air conditioners. (Surge resistor optional depending upon your genetic code.)

The Umbrella Lobe: I don't need to tell you that Florida leads the nation in frequency of skin cancer cases. Ultimately, this will lead to a massive, fleshy protuberance that will blossom from the top of the head and mushroom out to shade the entire body. The Umbrella Lobe will be impervious to harmful ultra-violet rays and will also come in handy during those surprise afternoon thundershowers. This should create a demand for a whole new line of both formal and casual body wear.

The Tune Slot: Gotta have music wherever we go. So, with the onset of puberty, certain Floridians will develop a vertical crevice along their sternums into which a compact disc can be inserted. Balance and volume controls will protrude along the collar bones, with speakers in each deltoid region.

These are absolutely necessary since we beach-going Floridians already have too much stuff to lug around with us and, besides, the sand and salt gum up the store-bought models. Those who evolve Tune Slots will never be without friends.

"Hey, Max, shove another disc into Pete, willya?"

"Open up, Pete. Thanks, pal."

Pete, of course, should be kept from extreme heat and will require occasional cleaning with Q-tips swabbed in rubbing alcohol.

Thigh-Paks: Another recreational necessity that will develop in those who don't come equipped with Tune Slots. Hinges will form at the lower buttocks and the rear of the knee, creating a handy, flip-open compartment that can be used to store up to a six-pack of 12-oz. beverages. (Dry storage available in large adults.)

Navigational Printout Node: Say you are walking down the street and up pulls this family in a station wagon and the Daddy asks: "Say, bub, can you tell me how to get to Sea World?" No more will you be inconvenienced. Located within your navel, the NPN can be activated by simply flexing the abdominal muscles. A micro-printer hooked directly to your pre-programmed navigational center (which makes constant allowances for your ever-changing location) will be able to give the wayward traveler the precise description of where he should go within seconds. It can be programmed to give elaborate – but wrong – directions to tourists you find annoying.

Those are just a few of the new, improved body parts you Floridians have to look forward to in the milleniums ahead.

So why are you just sitting there? Hurry up and evolve!

The New Me

. . . .

I LIKE THE NEW ME. THE NEW ME HAS A certain panache that was lacking in the Old Me. The New Me takes no guff.

The New Me was standing out in the front yard last Saturday watering the azaleas when along came two men and a little girl loaded down with religious pamphlets.

"This is Mary Ann," said one of the men, giving the little girl a gentle push my way. "If you have a few minutes she would like to speak with you."

And before I could explain that I didn't have a few minutes, that I wanted to stop watering the azaleas and go inside to watch the ballgame, Mary Ann was quoting some verse from the Book of Revelations and explaining how I, too, could find salvation.

The Old Me might have cut off Mary Ann. The Old Me might have told the three of them to be on their way. The Old Me might have had some fun with the water hose.

Not the New Me. The New Me waited until little Mary Ann had finished speaking her piece. (Who can interrupt a child, anyway? These annoying people know that. That's what gets me.)

"What time do you usually sit down to eat dinner in the evening?" I asked the man who had introduced me to Mary Ann.

"Oh, around 6:30," he said. "Why?"

"Do you have a business card?" I asked.

"Why, certainly," said the man, going for his wallet. "If you would be so kind as to write down your home address on it, along with any specific directions I might need for finding your house," I said.

The man stopped.

"Why?" he asked.

"Because I intend to drop by, maybe next week, while you are eating dinner, and tell you all about my religious beliefs. I will bring along my children. They have some very interesting beliefs as well, although they tend to get sort of whiny that time of day. Oh, please make sure you include your home phone number on that card, so I can call up on the days when I can't visit in person."

"I don't think that will be necessary," said the man, taking Mary Ann by the hand and turning to go.

"Oh, shoot," I said. "And I was hoping maybe you'd invite us in for dessert."

That is how the New Me operates.

Telephone solicitors? The Old Me cussed and hung up on them. The New Me cannot wait to get a call.

"Yes, I'm calling for the Police Benevolent Association and we're hoping we can count on you for a donation to our annual ... "

"My Uncle Smedley always wanted to be a policeman. Only he lost his left leg in that tragic incident with the bass trombone. He would have made a good policeman though ... "

"I'm sure he would have. Now, for just $35 you can purchase a ticket to our annual ball ... "

"Uncle Smedley wasn't much of a dancer. Except when he'd been drinking. When he'd been drinking couldn't anyone stop him from hopping out on the floor.

"Used to embarrass the dickens out of Aunt Zelma. Poor Aunt Zelma ... "

"Um, yes. Now, our annual ball will be on Nov. 23 this year and ... "

"My goodness. That is just five days before what would have been Uncle Smedley's 83rd birthday. What a coincidence. I can't wait to tell Aunt Zelma. Why ... hello ... hello?"

The New Me rejoices when telephone solicitors do the hanging up.

And those subscription cards that always fall into your lap when you are reading magazines? The Old Me used to just throw them away. The New Me understands that if I drop these cards into the mail then the magazines responsible for them will have to pay the postage.

Heh-heh.

I write notes on these lap-cards, knowing that they will be received by some poor schmoe in the subscription department mailroom who could sure use a lift.

"I'll pass on the subscription offer," I write.

"But I think that you, personally, are doing a great job with the

mail. Watch out for paper cuts!"
The New Me enjoys brightening the days of other people.

My kids? How does the New Me handle them? Well ...
"Daddy, when are you going to buy us Super Nintendo?"
"Listen, you've got regular Nintendo and if you think ... "
"When, Daddy, when?"
" ... is obviously just a devious marketing scheme to create a new layer of video game morons, then ... "
"Please, Daddy, please!"
" ... as soon as possible. Anything your little heart desires."
The New Me is still working on that one. OK?

The Old Man and the Boat

• •

THERE'S THIS HOUSE I DRIVE BY often and in its driveway there's a boat. The boat is for sale. It has been for sale for a long, long time.

Turns out I've been looking for a boat lately. But then my definition of "lately" is broader than most. Because I've been looking for a boat for, oh, about the last 15 years.

Even when I've owned perfectly good boats, of which there have been several, I would tell people: "Yeah, I've been looking for a boat lately."

There are worse things, such as the truth, to waste your time looking for.

Although . . . a boat with a kicker that will always crank when the lightning is bolting down around you and the waves are washing over the transom and you just know you are going to crash on the rocks and die even though you still owe lots of money on the boat and your children won't get to go to college and you could have cashed in your I.R.A. and accepted the penalty and lived high on the hog before you crashed on the rocks and died . . . that kind of boat, a boat you can count on, is far more elusive than the truth. Which is why people like me enjoy the challenge of looking for boats and to hell with the truth about them.

This particular boat for sale in the driveway of the house I drive by often is not exactly the kind of boat I've been looking for lately. But the other day I stopped to check it out anyway. Just to make sure. Because, like Everest, it was there.

The fellow who owned it was out of his house before I was out of my car, making pretty good time in my direction with his aluminum walker. Looked to be in his 70s. Wore khakis with rolled-up cuffs over his slip-on Keds. Wore a long-sleeved white shirt with the top button buttoned despite the June heat. Wore a straw hat, the kind with a window of green, see-through plastic in the front bill, like you find for sale at better bait shops everywhere.

Fact was, the old man was decked out for fishing although it was perfectly obvious he was not capable of it. He had to stop and catch his breath. He coughed. The walker shook. His face was red and creased and crusty with old skin cancers. And the sun coming down through the green plastic gave his features a mossy tint.

"Interested in the boat?" he asked.

"Been looking for a boat," I allowed, not about to let on I was interested. And in the manner of the shrewd and serious boat shopper I proceeded to inspect his craft rather than pay him much attention.

"You fish?" he asked. I nodded. Didn't say anything.

"Fish for anything in particular?" he asked.

"Little bit of everything," I told him.

"Bass?"

"I'm not real big on bass."

"Know what you mean about bass," he said. "Tell you about this one time, though. About bass. See me and my boy, Thomas, the youngest one, I got three sons, don't none of 'em live around here any more, we were out over to Lake George and ... "

The story went on for a good 10 minutes about how he and Thomas got into those Lake George bass one day. I was polite about listening. But I kept drifting off, trying to size up the boat. The motor didn't look all that bad. A 70-horsepower Evinrude. No dings in the prop. Well-greased. But the hull ...

"Trout?" he said.

"What's that?"

"You fish much trout?"

"Oh, you know," I said. "Here. There."

"Mosquito Lagoon," he said. "You getchya a bucktail jig, a red one, and keep it tipped off with shrimp and you can't hardly go wrong in Mosquito Lagoon. Why, this one time ... "

And he was off and running again.

It really wasn't the kind of boat I was looking for. But I kept on looking anyway. If you've got chronic boat lust then you will look at any boat. And enjoy yourself immensely while doing so.

Doesn't make a bit of difference what kind of boat it is. You can be looking at a crummy little dinghy with rotten gunwhales and barnacles all over the bottom and still you will find something about it that's appealing.

"Nice oarlocks," you'll find yourself saying, even though you have no intention, ever, in somebody else's lifetime, of rowing. Chronic boat lust is a pathetic affliction.

The old man stopped for a breath in his trout story. Coughed. I cut in.

"So how much you asking?"

"What's that?" he said.

"How much you asking for the boat?"

He seemed to suddenly remember why I had stopped at his house, why we were standing there.

"Oh ... seven-five," he said.

"Excuse me?"

"Seven-five," he repeated.

"Seven thousand five hundred?" I asked.

He nodded. Then he grinned.

I grinned, too. Indeed, it was everything I could do to keep from laughing. The boat I was looking at was worth twenty-five hundred, maybe three thousand tops. It hadn't been worth seven-five when it was new.

"Mister, I don't mind telling you this boat ain't been out in three years," he said. "Motor ain't even been cranked in two."

"Sounds like you're talkin' it down."

"That price is firm," he said.

And I believed him. Believed, too, that if I offered him seven-five, then he'd raise his price, in a heartbeat, to eight.

The old man didn't want to get rid of his boat any more than he wanted to get rid of his memories. No, he didn't get out on the water anymore. But he still went fishing ... went fishing for those of us who would see the boat, see the "For Sale" sign and stop so he could talk.

"Went tarpon fishing a little while back," I told him.

"Let me tell you about this tarpon," he said. "See, we was over to Homosassa and ... "

Tailor-made Shakedowns

A FEW WEEKS AGO I RECEIVED A NICE, FRIENDLY LETTER FROM the publisher of *Soldier of Fortune* telling me that my first copy of his magazine would arrive any day. He welcomed me as a new subscriber.

And *Soldier of Fortune* promptly appeared in my mailbox. So did a bill for $32, the price of one year's subscription.

Fair enough. Subscribe to a magazine, pay the bill. Only problem: I didn't subscribe to *Soldier of Fortune*, which calls itself "The Journal of Professional Adventurers" and which is heavy on stories about mercenaries in Africa and the latest war games in the California desert and the newest automatic weapons, flak jackets and bugging devices for the serious fighting man.

The way I figure it, someone is messing with me. They are messing with me by signing me up for magazine subscriptions that I do not want.

I have absolutely no interest or aptitude in anything entrepreneurial. Yet, I began receiving *INC.* magazine. I have no particular curiosity about the quaint customs and lifestyles of New Englanders. Yet, *Yankee* was mysteriously mailed to me.

Likewise, I have also become a subscriber to *Popular Mechanics*, *Fortune, Architectural Digest* and *Mademoiselle* through no wish of my own.

I have no idea who is messing with me. But I wasn't about to waste good time puzzling over it. I tore up all the bills the magazines sent me.

I did read some of the magazines. I especially liked *Soldier of Fortune*. The classifieds were great: "Ex-CIA operative seeks discreet position. Will go anywhere, do anything."

And so were the mail-order bumper-sticker ads: "Gun control means being able to hit your target" and "Peace through superior firepower."

Eventually, all the magazines sent me follow-up letters asking that they get paid. When the shakedown letter arrived from *Soldier of Fortune*, I was a bit concerned. I did not want to get on the bad side of people who probably keep bazookas in their basements. But the letter was anti-climatic.

"Dear sir," it said, "We have not yet received your $32 payment for *Soldier of Fortune*. We kindly request that you send a check or money order ... blah-blah-blah-blah ... " just like the letters from all the other magazines.

It shouldn't be like that. I mean, a magazine like *Soldier of Fortune* has a reputation to uphold. And a shakedown letter from them ought to read:

"Dear scum of the earth: You have exactly 24 hours to pay the $32. If payment is not received in that time, our crack team of commandos will initiate a full-scale assault on your home, employing state-of-the-art tactical weaponry and incendiary devices.

"Upon your capture, Captain Omega, the commando leader, will personally torture you with the infamous U.S. Marine Raider Stiletto, the knife that was forged in hell. We await your immediate response."

In fact, I think all magazines should make their shakedown letters reflect the image their publications strive to project. Since I have recently become an expert on the genre, I offer my free assistance. For instance:

From *National Geographic*: "Dear sir: In the few months that you have received our magazine you have no doubt been impressed with the wonderful photography we display in each issue. When you neglected time and again to pay your bill, we assigned one of our photographers to follow you around – surreptitiously, of course – for a few days. You might be interested in seeing some of the photos he brought back (see enclosure). We think your wife, your boss and the local police chief might be interested, too.

We suggest you pay us what you owe us, then sign up for a lifetime subscription – a mere $2,500. Only then will we destroy the negatives."

From *Consumer Reports*: "Dear purchasing unit: We have tested your credit rating against six other subscribers and found you to be lacking in several crucial areas. Further association with you is hazardous. Therefore, we are recalling your subscription until you pay."

From *People*: "Dear non-person: Princess Di pays her bills. Paul Newman pays his bills. So does Billy Joel, Shirley MacLaine, Sly Stallone, Prince, Steven Spielberg, Mick Jagger, the entire Kennedy family and the cast of *The Cosby Show*. Anyone who's anyone pays their bills. Don't you wish you were someone?"

From *Gentleman's Quarterly*: "Dear sir: This winter's gentleman will be dressed in a camel-hair polo coat, a cashmere equestrian sweater, shepherd's check trousers, a viyella shirt and antelope leather Italian shoes, all reflecting his good taste, refinement and, above all, good word.

"Considering your negligence in paying us, we rather suspect this letter finds you in a worn-out T-shirt and boxer shorts. N'est-ce pas?"

From *New Yorker*: "Dear sir: It was a lovely winter afternoon and, as is our custom on such days, we decided to take a stroll back to our subscription department, always enjoying a bit of conversation with our colleagues there, charming folks that they are, possessed with wondrous insights about our many subscribers.

"Imagine our amazement when, in the course of conversation (we had been commenting on the new Japanese exhibit at the Hawthorne Gallery) someone, we believe it was Mr. Dickson from Accounts Receivable, mentioned, quite discreetly, that you owed us – how shall we say? – some money. No offense, but please pay."

From *Reader's Digest*: "(Condensed from *New Yorker*) Sir: Pay."

Turtle Treasure

· ·

WE WERE WALKING THE dune line at Canaveral National Seashore, looking for old bottles that might contain treasure maps. My sons are big on buried treasure. They demand a major hunt whenever we visit the beach.

They usually find something, mainly because I plant it secretly – tea tins filled with pennies, shoe boxes that spill forth fake jewelry and play money.

But this time I had come unprepared and the boys were getting restless.

"Dad, are we going to find some buried treasure or not?" demanded Bo, the 5-year-old.

"I want to go home," whined Dash, who's almost 4.

And then we found the turtle nest.

"Lookit!" shouted Dash. "A bulldozer has been here."

The turtle's path from the ocean did resemble the trail of a half-track. It was an arc-shaped furrow with the nest, scooped out the size of a washtub, sitting at its crest.

Next to the nest was a survey stake with a red flag. Park rangers had put it there, along with a chicken wire cage to keep out predators. The date was marked on the stake. The turtle had dug her nest and laid her eggs just the night before.

There are moments in raising children that can be absolutely magic, moments when parents are permitted the pleasure of presenting their children with great revelations and seeing those revelations connect. You cannot plan these moments. They simply happen.

So we sat by the nest for a long time and talked about turtles. I am no authority, but I've had the good fortune to read books by two Floridians who are. Jack Rudloe's *Time of the Turtle* and Archie Carr's *The Turtle Handbook* are recommended to anyone who plans a trip to the beach during turtle nesting season.

I told my sons about the Seri Indians who live on the Gulf of California and believe the world began on the back of a giant sea turtle. As the legend goes, on her back grew plants, then animals and finally the first Seri Indians.

"Is that really how the world began, Dad?" Bo asked.

"What do you think?" I asked him.

Both boys shook their heads no. My sons, already the skeptics.

I told them how the Greek god Hermes is said to have made the first musical instrument, the lute, out of a turtle shell and used it to play songs that could cast spells on people. The boys thought that sounded pretty neat.

"Do you have any of his albums?" Dash asked.

I told them how there were once so many sea turtles in Florida that bakeries used to sell velvety pound cakes made out of turtle eggs (the whites of turtle eggs don't coagulate like the whites of chicken eggs) and restaurants had turtle egg pancakes on their menus.

"Let's go eat some of those pancakes," Bo said.

He and his brother didn't like it when I told him that the days of turtle egg pancakes were long gone, that sea turtles have been killed off in such numbers that some species face extinction. Nor did they like it when I told them how raccoons and ghost crabs dig up turtle nests and eat the eggs. Still they seemed to understand the law of survival it implied.

"Maybe the coons and crabs would die if they didn't eat the eggs, right?" Bo said.

They got a kick out of my own turtle adventure, about the time I accompanied a researcher on a moonlit patrol near Fort Myers Beach and found a turtle having trouble digging her nest. A shark had apparently bitten off one rear flipper. She let us help her dig the hole, then deposited her load – 119 eggs that hit the nest like steaming Ping-Pong balls.

And when I pointed to the nest beside us and told my boys that in another 60 or 70 days, a hundred or so baby turtles would crawl out and go scrambling toward the ocean they could hardly control their excitement.

"Let's stay right here all the way until then," said Dash.

And we just might have, too, if the thunderstorm hadn't cranked up. The boys patted the nest, said goodbye to the turtles-to-be and we hurried off.

"Did you find some buried treasure?" asked my wife when we rejoined her.

"Yeah," said Bo, "but we left it buried."

Call it turtle treasure, a rare and magic find indeed.

Trees I've Known

●●●●●●●●●●●●●●●●●●●●●●

WE ARE RAKING UP LEAVES IN THE front yard, my sons and I. They are mad at me for making them do this. They know it is the first stage of my master plan. First they learn to rake the leaves. Then mow the grass. Then trim the hedges. Then maybe even make the mortgage payment while dear old Dad relaxes as gentleman homeowner, lord o'er all he still owes the bank for.

It is not going well with the leaves. The wind keeps scattering the piles and more leaves keep falling from the cherry laurel tree that my neighbors with the immaculate lawns would love for me to cut down.

"Can we take a little break?" asks Dash, the 6-year-old.

Not a bad idea. So the three of us ease down against the trunk of the cherry laurel, looking out at the leaves left to rake.

"I hate trees," says Bo, the 7-year-old. "What good are they anyway?"

I'm a father. I can take a cue. I can sense that I am being offered one of those rare and wonderful opportunities to be profound, to share with my sons some of my vast experience and wisdom.

And so I tell them about all the good trees I have known.

I tell them about the guava tree that stood behind the house where I grew up in Lake County. I must have been 3 or 4, and I remember walking out into our yard after watching Captain Kangaroo one morning and looking at that tree and thinking: "I am big enough to climb that tree all by myself."

I only managed to climb a little way, no more than a couple of feet. But it didn't matter. I was up there. I had removed myself from Earth. And as I lay there, inspecting with new perspective all that was around me, I fell asleep.

I woke up to hear my mother calling me. She couldn't see me in the tree. I had separated myself from her, from our house, indeed, from everything I had been attached to. I was terrified, but at the same time exhilarated. I hopped down and ran inside. But I came back often. It was my "thinking tree."

Then there was the camphor tree in the front yard of my grandmother's house. Camphor trees are about the best climbing trees you can find. The limbs are profuse and start low to the ground and they snake and curve and curlicue like some sort of psychedelic jungle gym.

There was one limb – the Camel we called it – that had three big humps on it. A trio of kids could sit on that limb and with a fourth kid on the ground tugging at the end of the limb – well, let's just say I spent many a day lost in adventures while riding the Camel.

I tell them about my first tree house, built when I was in fifth grade in a giant live oak across the street from Jeff Cherry's house in Leesburg. I fell out of that tree and broke my left wrist. When Jeff's father came running out, he asked me what was wrong, and I screamed: "I broke my damn arm, and it hurts like hell!" It was the first time I had ever cussed in front of a grown-up. Mr. Cherry didn't say anything about it.

I tell them about the citrus groves where we played army, using green oranges for ammunition. God, I can still feel the sting from some of those direct hits.

I skip the part about how, in high school, I went parking with girlfriends in those same groves when the trees were heavy with blossoms and the whole world seemed full of sweetness. They'll learn about all that soon enough.

And then I tell them about a couple of palm trees on a beach at Captiva Island where their mother and I used to string up a hammock and watch sunsets.

Fine place that beach, those trees.

Then I remind them of the "bird tree." It was a dogwood in the back yard of the house where we used to live. It was in a small town on a river and we had a bird feeder in the dogwood that cost us a small fortune in seed. Sometimes we would just pull up chairs to the window and sit there and watch the birds come and go.

So I'm finished talking about trees, and the boys don't have much to say. They've been absolutely quiet while I rambled. I can tell that I have had a fatherly impact. I can tell this has been just a dandy example of "quality time."

"So is there anything else I can tell you about trees?" I ask.

They both give me big-time sighs.

"Yeah," says Bo. "How much are you paying us for raking all these leaves?"

"And how much longer do we have to rake them?" asks Dash.

We stand up and get to work. I might just cut down that cherry laurel tree.

Robert Eugene Hardwick

●●●●●●●●●●●●●●●●●●●●●●●●●●

THE FIRST TIME WE MET he opened the door at his house, took one look at me and asked: "Who the hell are you and what are you doing here?"

I introduced myself, then explained that his daughter had invited me to dinner so I could meet her parents.

"Well I didn't invite you," he said. "Get out of here."

Then he slammed the door.

I stood around for a moment, saw that the door wasn't being reopened, then let myself in.

He was sitting in the living room watching TV. He didn't even look at me when I walked into the room.

"If you want a drink, fix it yourself. The bar's over there," he said.

As I mixed one, a strong one, I heard him mumbling: "Breaks into my house, helps himself to my liquor. Next thing I know he'll be wanting to marry my daughter."

I waited a few months for that actually, but such was my introduction to the man who became my father-in-law.

Being a father-in-law is tricky business, I suppose, especially when it means giving your daughter in marriage to a man whose beliefs and opinions are so radically different from your own. It's a matter of pride.

Being a son-in-law is no easier, especially when the father-in-law in question is as hard-headed as they come. It, too, is a matter of pride.

We got into an argument that first night we met. He owned a Chrysler-Plymouth dealership and didn't like the fact that I drove a

Volkswagen van.

I offered the opinion that foreign cars were generally superior and car salesmen weren't to be trusted in the first place. It was a lovely evening.

From that point on, we rarely saw eye to eye on anything. And even if we did, we would never let the other know.

When he found out I was a die-hard Gator fan, he started rooting for the Seminoles. He loved stock-car racing, so I never missed an opportunity to point out the absurdity of grown men driving round and round in circles.

Shoot, we even argued about the clothes we wore. I poked fun at his double-knits and Italian shoes. He couldn't stand my rumpled cotton shirts, especially a certain pink button-down oxford I had a fondness for.

"Pinko," he said whenever he saw me in it.

But what we really did battle over was politics. He thought President Reagan could do no wrong. I thought President Reagan was ... well, let's just say I thought he was good for some laughs.

A couple of years ago, the Republicans came up with this fund-raising gimmick called the Presidential Task Force. Send in your money and you got a badge, a plaque, an autographed picture of President Reagan and even access to a hot line that you could call for information about "The Force." I thought it was hilarious and wrote a column that said the Presidential Task Force was much like Dick Tracy's Crimestoppers Club, the main difference being that the Crimestoppers Club had more capable leaders.

Well, of course, after that my father-in-law just had to join the Presidential Task Force. He made a point of hauling out his badge and his plaque whenever I came to visit. He even offered me his autographed picture of President Reagan. I'm afraid I was somewhat less than gracious in turning it down.

God, how we argued. We defined ourselves by how we differed. Through it all there was respect and, yes, love.

I guess it's obvious by now that I've been referring to my father-in-law in the past tense.

He died Monday morning. I was holding his hand when it happened. Like always, there was no arguing him out of it. He knew it was time to go and no one could tell him different.

The next day, I read his obituary in the newspaper.

It said Robert Eugene Hardwick was "a former automobile dealer, active in real estate and a member of the Presidential Task Force."

I couldn't help but laugh when I saw that last part.

"He insisted on putting that in there, just to get to you," my mother-in-law told me.

We buried him Wednesday. I stood by his daughter. Our two sons each put a rose on his coffin.

I wore my rumpled pink shirt. Just to get him ...

Goodbye to the Groves

●●●●●●●●●●●●●●●●●●●●●●●●

I GOT LOST IN AN ORANGE GROVE when I was 6 or 7. It was quite on purpose, mind you. I just wanted to get off and be by myself (a brother-sister spat prompted everything as I remember). And because a grove bordered one side of our house – this was in Lake County where groves used to border just about everything – it was the perfect sanctuary.

I didn't stay lost long. When my mother called I came running. But from then on I slipped off and wandered the grove every chance I got. It was green and orderly and comforting, yet filled with just enough mystery to fire a boy's imagination. I did a whole lot of imagining there.

There was another grove behind a friend's house. We played army in it. Green oranges made great hand grenades; rotten grapefruit, fine fragmentation bombs. There was a rule that you couldn't fire at the head or on anyone whose back was turned. There was honor in our grove wars.

I used to hunt arrowheads in a grove alongside U.S. Highway 27. No telling what might turn up after the tractors rolled through and churned the rows. I found a spearhead once, bigger than my hand.

As a Tenderfoot in Boy Scouts I was tricked by the older guys into going on a snipe hunt in an orange grove. I sat alone in that grove all night long, holding a paper sack and fully believing that a snipe would come running into it. I must have eaten 20 oranges just to pass the time. Did I ever feel the fool come morning.

I learned to drive in a grove, the one that surrounded my cousin's house. The two of us were hotshots – 14 years old and on wheels, grinding the gears and crashing through limbs and just generally brutalizing that old pickup.

Later, in that same grove, when the blossoms were narcotically sweet, I went parking with a girlfriend. Got stuck, of course, and had to call my father to come pull us out. Humility was something else I learned in the groves.

I worked in the groves too. I picked oranges and hoed weeds and, come threats of a hard freeze, I helped fire the heaters or burn the tires that warded off the cold. There is nothing like grove work to make you aspire to doing something better.

And then there were the grove parties. A bunch of us would get together in a grove that cozied up to Lake Harris. There would be a bonfire and bottles of bourbon. We would take slugs and chase them with bites from an orange. Then we would stay up half the night laughing and arguing and solving the problems of the world. God, were we ever free.

But, to steal a line from S.E. Hinton, that was then and this is now. The groves I grew up with are all gone. Back-to-back killer freezes, almost biblical in their vengeance, did in the groves. No chance for a rebound.

Where I once got lost, where I once played army, the trees have been bulldozed and burned. A mobile home park sits where I hunted arrowheads. The snipe-hunting grove – its trees bare as dry bones – sports a "for sale" sign. My cousins want to plant pine trees where their grove stood, maybe subdivide it somewhere down the road. The party grove already has gone that route.

I have heard it said that to be a Floridian is to live with a constant sense of loss. It is the nature of change in this state. But the passing of the groves from these parts is just too much losing. They were supposed to always be here. Always.

The financial setbacks have been tallied. But it is the psychic deprivation that will be more costly.

It is not unlike what happened in Florida some 50 years ago when they passed the fence laws and did away with the free range.

"It was like chipping off a chunk of your heart," Mitchell Hansell, a Cracker in Kissimmee once told me. "It was like all your heritage just going to hell."

Growers are planting new groves, but they are to the south and they are different. They are not as accessible, surrounded by irrigation canals and, thanks to citrus canker, barbed wire. The days of grove roaming are long gone.

Not too long ago, for the first time in my life, I went to the grocery store and actually bought a bag of oranges. Before, they were always free for the picking.

And in my fireplace, I burn orange wood, cut from a grove that is no more.

The fire is hot, its fragrance bitter – a heritage up in smoke.

Curse of the Cowlick

•••••••••••••••••••••

I WENT TO THE GROCERY STORE the other day, my 6-year-old son, Bo, along as sidekick. No sooner had we stepped inside than he made a mad dash for the water fountain.

He wasn't thirsty. He was making a statement. By the time I caught up with him, there was a puddle on the floor, runoff from the icy geyser that was soaking him smack on the crown of his head. He looked at me and put his head on spin-dry cycle, spraying droplets this way and that. Then he ran both hands straight back from his forehead, fingers combing those limp blond strands until they stood straight on end, like hair on a cat with its tail in a socket.

"This," announced Bo, "is how I want my hair."

I put my arm around him, drew him close in my best fatherly fashion and said: "I know, son, I know. But you have to understand there just ain't no way."

We are, you see, victims of the Cowlick Curse. I have one. He doesn't. It is a sorry trick dipped up from the genetic sludge pond. It condemns us both to sporting coiffures cruelly out of sync with our prospective generations. When I was young, I would have done most anything to have hair like my son's, hair free of all restraint, hair capable of cascading down my forehead, hair as straight and stringy as, well, as straight and stringy as the Beatles'. Before they made it on the scene I was content, as were my contemporaries, with a crewcut. Indeed, I have hair that is perfect for a crewcut. That's because it is not an ordinary cowlick that graces my head. No, the whole herd got in on this one. If the rest of my hair is wavy enough to make you seasick, then that cowlick is the sea wall. Nothing gets past it.

During that all-too-brief period of my adolescence when crewcuts, especially flattops, were in vogue, things were great. The other guys had to use Butch Wax to make their hair stand up. Me, I didn't have to do a thing. My hair not only stood up, but it also snapped to attention and saluted.

Then came the Beatles. Hair that stood up was out. I borrowed Butch Wax and tried to put my cowlick at ease, tried to coax it down. All I got was a greasy forehead. And more pimples.

I knew girls who ironed their hair to get it to do what they wanted. Let's just say I'm lucky that my self-inflicted burns were never worse than second-degree. The cowlick was singed, but undaunted.

For a time I thought it possible to overwhelm my cowlick with sheer bulk. If only I could get the rest of my hair long enough, then surely the cowlick would yield to the weight and forelocks would finally meet eyelashes. This was semisuccessful. Viewed full front, the effect was enough to fool the casual glance. Get any angle on it, though, and it was sort of like the grillwork on a '57 Chevy. It stuck out there.

There was another problem with growing hair long enough to conquer my cowlick – my father. He was, and still is, as committed to crewcuts as cods to cod liver. To this day he gives himself a weekly crewcut on the back porch.

Just when it seemed as if I was making real progress in hair length, he would plug in the electric shears, point to the wooden stool and say, "Sit down."

"Just around the ears, okay, Dad?" I'd tell him. "I'm trying to let it grow out."

"Sure," he would say. "No problem."

Then I would feel that razor plowing a path down the middle of my skull.

"Oops, slipped!" my dad would say. And it was back to Burr City for Bob.

So, yes, although I have reached a state of peaceful co-existence with my cowlick and the vagrant waves it strives to contain, (my hair style is much like President Reagan's recollection of the Iran-Contra affair: never the same each day), old feelings die hard.

I tell my son: "When I was a boy I wanted hair just like yours."

He, however, sees the likes of Brian Bosworth, Arnold Schwarzenegger and older kids with trendy, radical buzz cuts and knows the Cowlick Curse has delivered a reverse whammy by not granting him its presence. His hair just will not stand up. His is a natural Beatle.

I counseled him. We are what we are what we are, I said. And he almost fell for it. Until the other day when the doorbell rang and we opened it to find one of the neighborhood boys standing at the door, his long hair gone, a crewcut in its place.

"That's what I really want!" said Bo.

I am keeping him away from my father.

Bob's Bad Day

• • • • • • • • • • • • • •

I GOT UP EARLY IN THE MORNING, before the sun, went into the kitchen and started boiling water for coffee. I opened the refrigerator. No coffee.

I decided to drive to the 24-hour grocery store that always has everything. I went out to my car. My kids had been playing in the car the day before. They had left all the windows down. It had rained overnight. It's truly amazing how quickly mildew grows here in Florida, isn't it?

Also, a small, furry beast – maybe one of the cats, maybe a possum, maybe a gorilla, I dunno – had crawled into my car to get out of the rain. As a gesture of gratitude for the shelter, the small furry beast had left a little something behind.

Like I said, it was dark. I sat down in the seat. First, I noticed it was wet. Then I noticed the little something. Luckily, there was some typing paper in my back seat that I could use to clean up. I reached for it. What I want to know is this: Do paper companies actually hire people whose job it is to sharpen the edges of paper? And why can't this technology be used on my kitchen knives? Also, what is the most appropriate first aid for paper cuts?

I drove to the grocery store. At the precise moment I pulled into the parking lot, I realized I had forgotten my wallet. I drove home, got my wallet and on the way out the door I noticed the brown smudges I had left on the white tile in the hall. All I know is that the small furry beast must have been really, really grateful.

At the grocery store, my favorite brand of coffee was missing from the shelf.

"We'll be restocked by this afternoon," said the stockboy.

I feel bad now about what I said when he shared this information with me.

"By the way," the stockboy said, "you might want to check the seat of your pants."

I feel even worse about what I said then.

I pulled into my driveway. One of the cats ran out from the bushes. I hit the brakes. I heard something swishing around in the back of the car. Then I smelled it – chlorine. I'd left the pool chemicals in the car. Ah well, that brown carpet in the car was too dark anyway. It will look nice all bleached out.

On the way inside, I picked up the newspaper, marveling at my carrier's accuracy. His lifetime average is a very solid .938 percentage for hitting the standing water.

I went into the kitchen, turned on the oven and put the newspaper inside to dry out. That's when I noticed that I had left the water boiling for my favorite brand of coffee. Actually, all the water had long since boiled away and, instead of steam, these tiny silver balls were spurting out of the kettle. Melted Teflon, I suppose. The tiny, silver balls were going ping-ping-ping all over the stove top.

I grabbed the kettle and tossed it into the garbage pail. It is a plastic garbage pail. It is a plastic garbage pail that can withstand a molten-hot kettle for exactly 30 seconds. Then it melts and crumples.

I took everything and dumped it outside. I think the melted plastic will come out of my shirt. Eventually.

I went into my den. I sat down at my computer and started to write a column. It was a pretty good column. Matter of fact, it was a column that probably could win the Pulitzer Prize. Then the power went out. You know, I keep meaning to buy one of those gizmos that protects your computer when the power goes out. When the power came back on my column was gone. It was a great column. Take my word for it.

I decided to go through the mail. I opened a letter. It said: "This is a chain letter. It was started in 1967. In 1969, Agnes Johnson made 10 copies of this letter and mailed them to friends. Four days later she inherited $457,000. In 1977, Phil Goshorn ignored this letter. A week later he sailed to the Bahamas and has not been seen or heard from since. Act at once! If you fail to carry out the spirit of this letter and break the chain, then bad luck will befall you, too."

Ha! Double ha!

Come at me with all you've got. Torture me with paper cuts and inferior brands of coffee. Let small, furry beasts crawl into my bed. Let my newspaper carrier start aiming for the windows. Lay it all on me. I do not care.

But for now you'll have to excuse me. I smell something. How long do you usually cook your newspaper?

Farewell to a House

· ·

MY GRANDMOTHER lived alone there when I paid my first visits to the house. This was after my grandfather died and before we moved in to help take care of her. My grandmother was very deaf and very English. She refused to wear a hearing aid and took tea each afternoon at the dining room table. I liked to join her because it meant toast with homemade orange marmalade. She couldn't hear me unless I yelled in her ear. So mostly we just sat there and smiled across the table. We understood each other perfectly.

My grandmother cooked and cleaned and worked in the yard until she died at 91. My first memories of the house are the aromas she gave it: Butterscotch pie cooling on the kitchen counter. Plums and guavas, boiled and waiting to be turned into jelly. Vases full of magnolias in the spring, gardenias in the summer. And always the smell of Johnson's Wax, which was rubbed into the oak floors weekly and buffed to such a slick finish that, when grown-ups weren't watching, I would take off my shoes, get a good running start in my socks and, from the dining room all the way down the long hall to the front door, I would glide . . .

My father was born in the same upstairs bedroom that he and my mother moved into after we came to live with my grandmother. That was in 1957. I was in second grade and remember thinking: I, too, will grow old in this house.

It was a wonderful house in which to be a child. There was a goldfish pond out front, a giant camphor tree more challenging than any jungle gym and a side yard big enough for Sunday afternoon football games. There were 12 rooms, seven porches, six fireplaces, a cellar and I don't know how many closets – vast, dark and terrifying to explore. The staircase had a bannister you could slide down. And when Peter Barber came to visit and ran up the stairs he always skipped the 13th step for fear that something spooky would grab him. Our house, of course, was haunted.

Most haunted of all was the two-story turret that you entered through my parents' bedroom on the second floor. Once, opening the turret door, I looked down to find three dead bats on the floor. I slept with a light on for months. When I was in high school, I would sneak up to the turret alone. There, feeling quite on top of everything, I would smoke cigarettes, commune with family ghosts and wish the time would hurry up and come for me to get out of Leesburg.

It was a wonderful house to come home to, especially at Christmastime. There was a Steinway baby grand in the parlor and on Christmas Eve my mother and sister would take turns playing while we sang carols. Our big number was We Three Kings. My father, my brothers and I each took solos. Seasons passed. We added wives, husbands and children to the chorus. We sang loud. We sounded awful. Year after year after year ...

The ceilings were 12 feet tall. The room between the kitchen and the dining room was called the butler's pantry. There was a small button on the walls of most rooms so that servants could be summoned. My sister's bedroom was once the maid's quarters. There were no showers and the legs of the bathtubs were shaped like lion's paws. Pigeons had nests all along the roof. The walls were covered with cherry picture frames containing photographs of long-departed relatives I never knew, but whose names I repeated like a litany. As a kid, when I brought new friends home to play, they would stop dead in their tracks and say: "You mean you live here?"

Maybe my mother and father just got tired of living with all the ghosts. I don't know. The house got to be too much for them. The last time it was painted it cost $10,000. If this were the best of all possible worlds then their children could have told them: "Listen, we'll buy the house so you can have plenty to retire on, plus spend the $100,000 or so it will take to restore the place and keep it up." But it wasn't that way. They had to sell the house.

Shortly after the "For Sale" sign went up in the yard, the

Leesburg Heritage Society invited me to speak. They wanted me to talk about the house. But no sooner had I stepped to the podium than I started weeping. I couldn't finish speaking. I am weeping even as I write this ...

The most up-to-date chronology:

1892: Built by E.H. Mote, one of Leesburg's early mayors. 1908: Occupied by Bishop H.C. Morrison, a Methodist and founder of the church next door. 1917: Bought by John and May Morris. 1974: Listed upon the National Register of Historic Places. 1988: Sold by Robert and Georgiana Morris to Morrison Memorial Methodist Church.

On the night before the closing, one year ago this weekend, we camped out in the house, my brothers and I. All the furniture was gone, divvied up among the family. The house moaned with emptiness. We stretched out sleeping bags on the parlor floor. We plugged in the old Bell & Howell projector and watched some ancient home movies. We laughed and told stories and drank too much bourbon. After my brothers fell asleep, I roamed the house. I stood in the middle of each room and tried to soak up, to remember, each and every thing that happened there. Morning came too soon. I left in a hurry and have not been back inside since.

The church wants the house gone. They want to build a brand new Sunday school building where the house stands, maybe a parking lot. It is their house, no longer our house. I joined up with some folks who started a preservation group to stop the church from tearing it down. We made signs and picketed the church one Sunday during services. On his way inside to worship, the father of one of my oldest friends stopped to talk. "You know there is nothing special about that house, historically or architecturally. It is just old and falling down. Besides, if you really wanted to save it, then why didn't you buy it?" he said. "You're just standing in the way of the Lord's work."

There was nothing I could have said that would have made any difference. The Lord, I know, works in some damn strange ways.

Now there's talk of moving the house to a vacant lot across Main Street, maybe turning it into a local historical museum. The preservationist group and the church are working together on it. It pains me to think of moving the house, but it pains me more to think of it torn down.

I keep telling myself: It is no longer our house; it will always be our house. But that's too Zen for me.

Here is what I know: This is the way of Florida. You live each day with a constant sense of loss. And nothing says you have to like it.

Campy Camping Tips

• •

I AM DELIGHTED THAT MORE and more American families are spending their summer vacations camping. Makes it easier for the rest of us vacationers to get motel rooms without reservations.

Just joking. As a former Boy Scout and one who earned merit badges for such outdoorsy things as "Latrine Sabotaging," "Insect Squashing" and "Whittling Semi-Lethal Weapons Out of Tree Branches," I have an abiding fondness for camping. Why, I could easily say that my experiences as a scout helped mold the deep love of nature and the outdoors that I enjoy today.

Of course, I could just as easily say that dissecting a frog in ninth grade biology class helped me become a brain surgeon. It would be a horrible lie. And, truth is, any love I possess for nature and the outdoors was probably molded by "Wonderful World of Disney" documentaries and old *National Geographic* magazines.

Still, Boy Scout camping trips did teach me a number of Outdoor Survival techniques. And, with the vacation season upon us, I am pleased to share some of them with you today in hopes that you may enjoy the great outdoors like I did that wonderful summer at dear old Camp La-No-Chee, which took its name from the Seminole Indian word for "Place where parents send their kids for a week to get some peace and quiet around the house."

This was the summer that an armadillo ate my underwear. Don't ask me how it got in the tent. The armadillo, that is. My underwear belonged in the tent and was neatly stashed away where it was supposed to be – in a cereal box.

Now, you beginning campers might not understand why it was necessary for a skilled outdoorsboy, like myself, to keep his underwear in a cereal box on a camping trip. But you must remember that it is often dark in a tent. Especially when your flashlight batteries corrode after the first night and your eyes are swollen shut from bug bites or poison ivy or your having mistakenly eaten the 6-12 stick-on repellent thinking it was a Baby Ruth bar. If you cannot locate your backpack in the dark, then you must improvise.

That's what camping is all about, really. Improvising. Making use of what is at hand. Living off the land. And those who are really accomplished at it probably remove the cereal before they stuff dirty underwear in a cereal box.

Anyway, the armadillo, who was only responding to basic, savage instincts and a fondness for Cheerios, seemed happy with his discovery and was last seen rooting toward the woods with some size 16 Hanes jockey shorts over his snout. I certainly didn't miss the underwear which, like all clothing you wear on a camping trip, had taken on a life of its own and, earlier that day, had completed a five-mile hike by itself. And I never told Billy Barwick, my tentmate, exactly where the armadillo had found my underwear since Billy always seemed to be munching on what was left of the Cheerios whenever I thought about bringing it up.

So for all of you who wish to avoid similar wardrobe thefts by marauding woodland creatures, the best thing to do with your underwear on a camping trip is: Don't wear any. This helps you get just a little bit closer to nature.

Also, I would strongly suggest that:

1. You don't forget to pack toilet paper.

2. After you forget to pack toilet paper then don't, under any circumstances, attempt to improvise and live off the land by substituting Spanish Moss, since it will generally take at least a week for the chigger bites to stop itching.

Other random Outdoor Survival hints that might prove helpful:

• Always carry a snakebite kit. Not only will it amuse venomous reptiles, but in the event of a snake bite you can entertain the victim by making neat thwocking noises with the two little rubber suction devices.

• Always pitch your tent in a wide, open space. The TV reception is generally better.

• Always carry a compass. And keep it hanging from a handy clasp attached to your belt. That way when other outdoorspeople pass you in the woods they will be able to immediately identify you as a complete wonk.

- Always carry binoculars. That way you can observe, close at hand, how much trouble neighboring campers are having setting up their tents.

- In the event that you do get lost, then by all means remain calm. A human being can exist up to two weeks without food, and if you are found, you will be able to wear lots of old clothes you had grown out of.

- Learn some knots. Here are two basic ones:

Slip knot – An essential mountain climbing knot and good for tying things that you might want to unleash in a hurry, such as your children.

Square knot – Good for tying up people who actually suggest you should sing "Kum Ba Yah" around the campfire.

- Do not feed the bears. But it is considered a friendly gesture to at least offer them a beer.

- Leave only footprints. Unless you are on crutches from the bear attack.

- Take only memories. Unless you'd just as soon forget.

A Fine Floridian

●●●●●●●●●●●●●●●●●●●●●●●●●

IT ALL GOT STARTED IN THE supermarket checkout line the other day when the woman in front of me dropped a bell pepper on the floor. She had her hands full, so I picked it up for her.

"Thanks," she said. She paused, then said: "Isn't it just lovely out today?"

"Sure is," I said.

It was one of those days straight out of everyone's Florida Dream, wintertime and miserable most everywhere else, but here – upper 70s, not a cloud to be found and the breeze was blowing just right.

It was one of those Florida days that can be best appreciated by Floridians when it is described as "North Carolina in August." For all those summer days you wilted from the clinging, peninsular humidity that the word "sultry" does not even begin to define, envious of acquaintances with cool mountain retreats outside of Highlands or Hendersonville, this was the payoff.

It was one of those Florida days that makes liars out of those who say we don't have a change of seasons. Shoot, down here during winter the season is changing ALL the time. One day it's wet and cool and miserable. The next day it's spring. Keeps happening over and over again. We don't abide waiting on some complacent equinox.

It was one of those days when the azaleas had been tricked into blooming early, the kids were playing in the pool, my wife was in a chaise longue with a book, and I was thinking maybe something cool with rum might taste nice. I had gone to the supermarket for limes.

You know how it is with those kind of Florida days. Infectious. The woman in front of me had a bad case of it, too.

"I just love it down here," she said. "Can't wait until we finally move down for good."

I asked where she was from and we got to talking. The checkout line was bogged down anyway. And in no time at all I found out that she and her husband were planning to retire here from New York in a couple of years, that they loved fishing and golfing and were having the time of their lives on this trip. I mean, here was a woman who could have stepped right out of a Florida Division of Tourism commercial.

"You've got it good here," she told me when I let on I was a native.

Now admittedly, I am one of those natives who cringes at the mere thought of anyone else moving down here. I slipped into a blue funk when the last census report was released. More than 13 million of us on this narrow spit of sand? The fourth largest state, with a not-so-distant vision of out-populating, zounds, New York?

There is no stopping it. And because there is no stopping it, I do try to get along with newcomers. Really I do. And I get along real well with people like the woman in the supermarket.

In fact, let some newcomer wax eloquent about the good things in Florida and I'll wax right along with them. Sure, there's plenty wrong. But it's home. I like it here. And I like it when other people like it here.

So the two of us were going on about the good things in Florida when, from behind me, I heard a man say: "So where in New York ya from anyway?"

The man was in his 60s I'd guess. Just dying to cut in on our conversation.

"Ossining," said the woman.

"Albany," said the man. "And as far as I'm concerned there's only one thing good about this damn place – the weather. You can have everything else. Everything else ... bahhhh."

I just nodded and smiled at the man, hoping maybe he'd melt into the linoleum. The woman did the same thing. I was all set to talk to her some more but Mr. Albany was not to be denied.

"I been down here six years and this place isn't what it's cracked up to be," he said. "First, you got your roads. Not enough of them. And what roads you got are lousy. They don't know how to build roads down here like they do back home. Used to be they had low taxes down here. Not anymore. Then you got your rip-off artists. Everyone who is from Florida is just out to rip off everyone else. Then you got ... "

The guy was on a roll.

By the time he got finished we had heard the whole litany of what he didn't like, everything from bugs to mildew to the absence of mountains. Uh-huh. The guy actually complained about Florida being flat. As if geography was a simple matter of legislation or popular vote.

It doesn't do any good even talking to people like this. You cannot tell them a thing. So I just stood there thinking about what I would like to tell him. It is not possible to share it here.

But the woman, bless her, looked at me and, with just the right lacing of irony, said: "Isn't it lovely out today?"

She winked when she said it. I laughed.

"Sure is," I said. "Sure is."

It went right over the man's head. Jerks like him are stunning in their density.

"So when ya going back up to Ossining?" he asked the woman as she paid for her groceries and headed for the door.

She turned and looked straight at him.

"Oh, next week, unfortunately," she said. Then added with perfect timing: "And you are welcome to follow me if you've forgotten the way."

She smiled ever so sweetly. Then she was gone.

I couldn't bear to turn and look at the man. For all I know he actually did melt into the linoleum.

But I like that woman. Whoever she was. I like her a lot. She's going to make one fine Floridian.

Eating Trees

●●●●●●●●●●●●●●●●●●

THE PRIEST BROTHERS GREW UP eating rocks and trees, which is altogether better than it sounds. Indeed, it was typical table fare for any Florida cracker on a hardscrabble budget. All it took was easy access to salt water and the muscle to swing an ax.

The rocks were oysters, hauled in from the Gulf flats. The trees were sabal palms, Florida's state tree and the blessed provider of swamp cabbage.

The Priest brothers could hold their own when gathering rocks. But they had no match in trimming trees.

"When we was younger we could lay down a tree a minute," said Wayne, 58.

"When we was younger we had to lay down a tree a minute," said Dean, 64. "That was how we made our spending money."

Red Level, a community of maybe 100 people, sits a few miles north of Crystal River on U.S. Highway 19. It has been home to Priests for more than 200 years. At the cemetery there are headstones for Priests who died here in the 1780s. Likely it was a Priest who gave the community its name.

After traveling across the sand hills and scrub of North Florida, they found this broad, flat plain that cozies up to the Gulf's salt marshes. When they plowed the soil they noticed its reddish tint. The Priests planned to put down permanent roots here. It's only fitting that this community took its name from the soil – Red Level.

Priests first took title to land here in 1835. A 100-acre parcel of it remains. Dean and his wife live on one corner, Wayne and his wife on another. Their children have places there, too.

The outside is closing in on the Priests. To the south around

Crystal River and Inverness, mobile home parks and developments have sprung up so fast that U.S. 19 to St. Petersburg and U.S. Highway 41 to Tampa soon will be 90-mile corridors solid with people. About three miles west of Red Level sits Florida Power's nuclear plant, its twin cooling towers 50 times the height of any cabbage palm that's ready for eating.

Dean works at the plant. Wayne is retired from the Air Force. Like their forebears they raise a few head of cattle. They also run a custom meat-cutting business.

And from time to time, when they get an order for it, the Priest brothers load their axes into a pickup truck and go out cutting swamp cabbage.

When they were kids, they sold swamp cabbages for 10 cents apiece. Now they sell for $2 to $6 apiece, "depending on how much we like the customer and how much aggravation we had to go through to get the cabbage," Dean said.

The worst aggravation is in the summer, not only from the heat, but from the hornets and yellow jackets that nest in sabal palms.

The boots (the Y-shaped part of the frond that attaches to the tree) are like rubber and the outer layers of the palm are so spongy that the ax bite disappears. It takes determined yanking – the boots are stringy and stubborn – to make progress. Felling the tree is not so much an act of cutting as it is unwrapping.

Many a Floridian has been whipped by a sabal palm. Not too long ago I passed a plot of land along the highway where the bulldozers had been busy making way for yet another strip mall. Three or four dozen palms lay in a heap to the side.

"We're getting ready to burn 'em," the site foreman told me. "But if you want to cut yourself out some swamp cabbage then you are welcome to borrow my ax."

Mind you, the trees were already felled. And still it took me the better part of an hour to trim out the trunk, whittling it down to a yard-long stalk of swamp cabbage about as big around as a large man's lower leg.

The Priest brothers, working together, can finish the whole job in about 10 minutes. Their axes bite in counterpoint without a wasted stroke.

After the tree is down, their cattle swarm up to the stump and eat of the heart that remains.

The tree is dead. It won't sprout back. And yes, it is painful to think that an entire tree must be killed for a small hunk of heart that, boiled down, will feed eight to 10 people at the most.

The Priest brothers don't think sabal palms are in any danger of being killed off. Cold, drought and pestilence don't seem to bother the tree. Bulldoze a piece of land and, if it's not covered with asphalt, swamp cabbage will be growing thick six months later. Still, the state prohibits the cutting of sabal palm unless you do the cutting on your own land.

Just as there's a science to cutting the sabal palm, there's an art to cooking its heart. I like it fine raw, much like sweet celery. Classic swamp cabbage is boiled slowly with ham hocks or bacon. And it's worth the drive to Cedar Key to sample the local version of Heart of Palm Salad, which comes topped with a peanut butter ice cream.

The Priest brothers prefer swamp cabbage in even more exotic fashion. They eat squirrel and swamp cabbage, oysters and swamp cabbage.

Their favorite, though, is swamp cabbage and dumplings.

Let Dean have the last word on just how good it is: "You just roll them dumplings out like you would for chicken and dumplings and drop them in the cabbage. The dumplings soak up all that cabbage juice and, my God, it's so good it would make a bulldog go spit in a wildcat's eye."

Tunneling for Fritters

YEARS FROM NOW, IN the fairly distant future, when the Gulf Stream Tunnel has long since been completed and Floridians can just pack up and drive to the Bahamas any time they damn well please, schoolchildren will be asked this question on history tests: "Can you name the main reason the Gulf Stream Tunnel was built?"

And they'll all roll their eyes and say, "Sheesh, that's easy." The answer will be as well known to them as: "What were the Spanish conquistadors looking for when they plundered Central America?" (Correct answer: Pepto-Bismol); and "Why did the U.S. invade Canada in 1997?" (Correct answer: Convenience.)

The students will write down the correct answer to the Gulf Stream Tunnel question, which will be: "Conch fritters."

Or maybe it will be an essay question: "Explain why the Gulf Stream Tunnel was built." In which case, all the kids will roll their eyes and complain, because essay questions, even in the fairly distant future, will still be the pits. And then they'll write: "Because some man wanted conch fritters." I have a suspicion that, come even the not-so distant future, a single sentence beginning with a conjunction will be considered an essay.

But if there's any justice remaining in the world, the teacher will award only half credit for that answer and scribble across the test paper: "Be specific!" Having dreamed up the idea of the Gulf Stream Tunnel, I would like to be remembered as more than just "some man." Besides, they just happened to be the best conch fritters in the Universe.

When I was in the Bahamas a few months ago and had an hour to kill before the flight home, I hired a cab and told the driver: "Take me to find some conch fritters."

The driver's name was George LaMont. The card he handed me said: "For all your Bahama taxi pleasures, call on George LaMont, the Passenger's Friend." He had a boom box swinging from the rearview mirror. And the backseat of his taxi was unlike the backseat of any other taxi I have ever seen. From the floor, halfway to the ceiling, it was filled with . . . shoes. All kinds of shoes. Dress shoes. Sneakers. Sandals. Occasionally, George LaMont would pull up to groups of Bahamians standing on street corners. They would stick their heads in the windows and look at the shoes. Then they would step back and George LaMont would drive away. I can only assume he was trying to sell them the shoes. We didn't talk about it. For all I know, in addition to being the Passenger's Friend, George LaMont could also be owner of the World's Only Free Mobile Shoe Museum.

Eventually we arrived at the conch fritter stand. It consisted of an old woman sitting under a tarpaulin on an otherwise empty lot along a back street in a shabby part of town. A cast iron frying pan filled with grease sat atop a Coleman stove. Just like those barbecue joints you sometimes find in the most grimy, unlikely spots, as a source of conch fritters, this place looked immediately promising.

"Two dollar bag?" the woman asked. I shook my head yes. She turned on the stove and started cooking.

When she had finished I was holding a medium-sized grocery bag filled with conch fritters. Must have been 50 of them. Grease fairly dripped from the bottom of the bag. Large chunks of conch meat jutted out of each fritter. I ate one. It had long been my quest to find the Best Conch Fritter in the Universe. And at that precise moment I did. In the presence of perfection I could not speak. I smiled at the woman. She smiled back. Hers was what you might call a beatific smile. She knew she had the Best Conch Fritters in the Universe. Nothing more needed to be said.

George asked the woman if she wanted to look at some shoes. She told him, no, she had work to do. Then she turned off the stove and sat down. She was already napping by the time we drove off.

On the way to the airport, George was too busy helping me eat all the conch fritters to stop and let anyone examine his backseat full of shoes. Still, we couldn't finish them all. Along with a tip, I gave George a couple of fritters for the road.

"Anything to declare?" asked the customs agent as I was getting ready to board the plane.

"Conch fritters," I said, holding up the bag, which by this time was almost transparent with grease.

"They cannot leave the country," said the customs agent.

"Fine by me," I said.

I ate the last half dozen standing there. The customs agent said, no thank you, he didn't care for any. But he was nice enough to get rid of the bag.

I cannot justify buying an airplane ticket and flying all the way to the Bahamas just to eat conch fritters. Actually, I can justify it. Quite easily. But I'd feel guilty about it. And I don't want to book passage on a cruise ship. Ever. To anywhere.

What I would like to do is get in my van, drive to somewhere around Fort Lauderdale, enter the Gulf Stream Tunnel and, an hour or so later (Hey, it's only 70 miles) pop up in the Bahamas. As a Floridian, this seems a perfectly reasonable expectation.

Half-a-century ago we extended U.S. 1 all the way to Key West, building the Seven-Mile Bridge, the longest "continuous precast prestressed segmental bridge in the world." Surely, we've evolved enough by now to pull off the Gulf Stream Tunnel.

We can't let the British and the French outdo us. They have just completed the "Chunnel," the tunnel that connects those two nations under the English Channel. It is 47 miles long and now ranks as the single most spectacular feat of engineering on the planet. Here's our chance to beat it.

I telephoned London and the office of Eurotunnel, the company that built the Chunnel. I spoke to a nice woman named Allison who said she was an executive vice-president for strategic planning.

"Congratulations on building the Chunnel," I told her. "But over here in Florida we now have plans to outdo you."

I told her about the Gulf Stream Tunnel.

"You must be quite daft," said Allison.

"Daft" is one of those quaint words the British have so many of. It means "brilliant."

Yes, I am quite daft, thank you. Also, a little hungry for another conch fritter.

Heaps o' History

THE BEST THING TO DO ON any vacation through the United States is to spend the first couple of days exposing yourself to history, which in most progressive states is still only a misdemeanor.

Exposing yourself to history is a lot like getting a vaccination and exposing yourself to smallpox. It doesn't hurt much and once it's over you can relax, doing the things you were meant to do on vacation, such as sitting around motel rooms in your underwear and enjoying free HBO with the air conditioner cranked down 20 degrees lower than you would ever dream of running it at home. I decided to catch some history at Jamestown, Va., because it has three major things going for it:

1. Lots of people died there. And as most historians will confirm, the more dead people involved, the higher your quality of history.

2. It has a fort. Which means my kids could run around pretending to shoot guns and creating more dead people, thereby expending enough energy to maybe stop beating up on each other in the back seat of the car.

3. You can drive your car onto a ferryboat to get there. Which means I could get out of the car before I started beating up on the kids in the back seat.

I was standing at the rail of the ferry, observing the vast deposits of raw history that were getting closer and closer on the opposing shore, trying to put it all into a meaningful perspective, when I was approached by a man in his 60s who was wearing a shiny suit.

Him: "Beautiful countryside isn't it?"

Me: "Sure is."

Him (handing me his business card): "If you are ever interested in buying some real estate locally, then please feel free to call."

Me: "Why, thank you very much."

Him: "I suggest waterfront if you can afford it because it is steadily increasing in value."

Too bad he wasn't around in 1607 to explain this to the brave English settlers who came here looking for things of value, like gold and silver, but found malaria instead. They also found Indians, one of whom was Pocahontas, the Indian maiden who saved Captain John Smith from getting killed by her father, the Indian chief. Do you believe that story? Ha! You have obviously never been to Jamestown or else you would have learned that it is just one more colorful – but entirely bogus – legend that we Americans have dreamed up about ourselves, like that whopper about George Washington throwing a silver dollar across the Potomac River (it was a subway token actually).

What really happened was that the English, who were all very well-to-do gentlemen, and therefore unable to farm or forage or fend for themselves, held Pocahontas hostage until the Indians coughed up some provisions. Also, one of the Englishmen claimed Pocahontas as his bride and took her back to England. She was 12 at the time. This is true history. Look it up.

Also while in Jamestown I watched an Indian making an authentic bow and arrow. In all truthfulness, I must tell you that this Indian was probably just a history grad student in desperate need of employment, but like everyone else at Jamestown he was seriously pretending to be living in the 17th century. I asked him how long it took to make a bow and arrow, and he replied: "I just got finished explaining that if only you had been listening." So I assume he was playing the role of the grouchy Indian who lost his 12-year-old girlfriend to an Englishman.

Getting into the car after leaving Jamestown, I was approached by a local native who was pretending to be an authentic Helpful Person.

Him: "Hey there! How would you and your family like to be treated to a free smorgasbord dinner?"

Me: "What's the gimmick?"

Him: "Just pay a short visit to Jamestown Plantation, a brand-new condominium resort just down the road."

Me: "Listen, I'm from Florida. I've been vaccinated against condo salesmen."

Him: "Nice talking to you."

Still, I would have to say that our visit to Jamestown was very educational – the most important historical thing I learned being that the brave English settlers really blew it by not investing heavily in real estate.

Capital Line-up

I PROPOSE WE ERECT A monument that honors the good and decent citizens who flock to Washington, D.C., each year to witness up close, up extremely close, all scrunched up together even, Our Nation's Capital.

You know the Lincoln Memorial? You know how it shows Abraham Lincoln sitting? This new monument would contrast very nicely. It would depict hundreds, maybe thousands, of people standing. Standing in a line. A line that also is populated with small, antsy children whose lips you'll be able to read as they say such cute, endearing things as: "I like it better back at the motel" and "Right now! I have to go right now!"

I realize that Washington is not the only place where people stand in long lines to see the attractions. I realize that some world-class line standing goes on at Walt Disney World where, even as you read this, some pitiful family of four from Tullahoma, Tenn., where they don't ever stand in line for anything except potluck suppers at church, is approaching the sign outside Space Mountain that says "Two hours' wait from this point" and thinking: "My, how we will treasure this vacation memory." The difference in Washington is that people stand in line out of a deep, abiding patriotic conviction. (Translation: There's no admission charge to most places.)

Also, in Washington standing in line becomes a very sensory experience. Especially at the Washington Monument, where you stand in a line that circles an obelisk I feel certain was secretly designed to concentrate the sun's harshest rays so that you can enjoy one of our many inalienable rights – the freedom to perspire copiously in public. Then about 50 of you are herded into an elevator and made to stand right next to each other for what turns out to be a very long ride to the top during which most people practice breathing through their mouths. Call it treason, but I'll say it anyway – the Washington Monument has terminal b.o.

Some of the lines in Washington do move quickly and don't smell all that bad, like the one at the National Archives, where they keep the Declaration of Independence and the Constitution in a glass case. Yes, these treasured documents are on view for all freedom-loving humans to see just so long as you don't actually stop to look at them. There are two guards flanking the glass case and their job is to alternate saying, "Keep moving!" and "Don't stop!" so that the line moves quickly toward a gift shop, where reasonably priced facsimiles can be purchased and looked at in a stationary position. To heighten authenticity and at a small additional price you may buy a cassette tape of the guards barking orders.

Other lines not to be missed include those outside the Capitol and the White House which, if you are in luck, will be composed of several thousand members of safety patrols from public schools throughout America all wearing their tasteful, fluorescent safety patrol belts and behaving like you would behave if you were 12 years old and on your first trip away from home without your parents.

But far and away the most interesting line I stood in while visiting Washington recently was the line outside the men's room at a pizza restaurant called the Zebra Room, a place that qualifies as a historic attraction because a former speaker of the House, while under the influence of lobbyists, once drove his car through the front door.

Actually, the real line was outside the women's room, where maybe a dozen women were waiting their turns when I walked up. I was headed for the men's room door, but stopped when one of the women stepped in front of me and announced to all, "To heck with waiting for ours, I'm going in here," and walked inside the men's room. A few seconds later, the guy who was using the men's room walked out, thoroughly baffled, another woman walked in and I proceeded to be a participant in what I guess might be called the unisexing of a public facility.

"They do this all the time in New York City," said the woman ahead of me in line.

"I'm going to start doing it in Atlanta where I live," said another woman.

Obviously this is one of your latest social trends regarding standing in line. It is heading south. Just thought you should be prepared.

Welcome to Nowheresville

••

THE CAR PULLED UP BEHIND ME AS I STOOD ON THE ROCKS looking out on Florida Bay. It was almost dark, but the sky was still garishly aglow, as if some wanton watercolorist had gone wild. After a while, the locals say, you stop noticing the sunsets. A sadder form of selective blindness I cannot imagine.

The driver, a middle-aged, shirtless man, whirred down the window and asked: "Which way to the restaurant?"

"There isn't a restaurant," I told him. "Closed for the summer."

"How about the grocery store?" he asked.

"No grocery store," I said. "They sell a few things at the marina, but it closed a couple of hours ago."

The man looked all around – salt marsh on three sides, Florida Bay stretching out to the south.

"I thought there was more here than just this. Drive all the way out here and . . . " He shook his head, then was gone the way he came. I resisted all temptation to feel smug. Just a few hours earlier, I had arrived in Flamingo for the first time and had thought the very same thing: Where is everything?

Not that I had expected, or even wanted, a whole lot. If anything, I was relieved to find so little. But you look at Flamingo on the map, a speck in the Everglades at the end of State Road 27, the southernmost mainland outpost in this, the southernmost mainland state, 45 miles away from any other town and even then it's only Homestead, and, if you are acquainted with the rest of Florida, then you just naturally conjure up certain images. Maybe some weathered fishing shacks left standing more for picturesque value than usefulness. An open-air bar with an unseemly Polynesian theme. At the very least, a Circle K, a 7-Eleven or both. And can you think of anywhere that doesn't have a video shop?

Welcome to Flamingo, where the National Park Service runs things and there's very little that needs running. It's a popular place in the winter. But come summer, thanks both to fewer visitors and recent park-service budget cuts, it's rare to even find a ranger at the two-story Flamingo station. A private company operates the marina and the only motel, the Flamingo Lodge. This time of year, the 20 or so employees generally outnumber the guests. At the campground, the prime waterfront spots that go for $10 a night in the winter are free until October. Still, nary a tent was pitched the entire time I was there. Looking for Nowheresville, Fla.? Anymore, this is as close as it gets.

So what do you do here? If you have to ask that question, you shouldn't even come. What I did was combat the world-class mosquito population, hunker down with some good books and make sure my bodily fluids never dipped too low, which is another way of saying I drank large quantities of water, beer and rum, in that order. It's the heat, don't you know.

And I caught fish. I am not a particularly accomplished fisherman and so I guess it is fitting irony that I should have my most glorious fishing experiences without benefit of a witness. Take my word for it.

First day out I rented a skiff and headed north to Whitewater Bay, part of the Wilderness Waterway, a 100-mile canoe trail that runs from Everglades City south to Flamingo. I started fishing with two lines out, but it was too much work. I kept six big trout and threw all the rest – I lost count – back. I saw four other boats all day long.

The next day I paddled my canoe 2 miles out on Florida Bay to Murray Key. Excitement is catching black tip sharks in a canoe in less than 2 feet of water. Got pulled all over the bay.

The day after that I paddled out again, this time with a cast net, and hauled in some mullet. Monster redfish were attacking the mullet and I managed to hook a few on silver spoons. Seldom have I fought fish until my arms grew tired. I wore plain out.

As I dragged the canoe ashore, a man got out of a car and walked up to me.

"Not much here, is there?" he said.

"Nope," I said, "not much at all."

"Thank God," he said.

Now there was someone who was going to like Flamingo. Then again, he might even love it.

Biblical BBQ

WHAT SADDENS ME ABOUT THE Fourth of July is how Americans have lost sight of why we observe this holiday. We've been deluded into honoring the accomplishments of some raging malcontents who, for merely signing a petition, came to be known as the Founding Fathers. As a result, millions of Americans will join today and celebrate independence. They will wave the flag and listen to Sousa marches and ooh-ahh to fireworks. Few among them will stop to think about the true spirit of the Fourth of July.

I am talking about the spirit symbolized by a miracle that signaled the beginning of modern civilization. It was an event that inspired one of the world's great religions. I refer, of course, to the Birth of Barbecue.

Say hallelujah!

And so I would ask that you take a few moments today amid all the frivolity to remember the Barbecue Story:

The Beginning: In the Beginning there was only a void. Indeed, all was but a pit. An open pit.

But it was not good, for there was no charcoal. Nor were there long-handled tongs or basting brushes or silly aprons that said, "Kiss Me I'm the Cook."

There were, however, some ribs. But they were in use, and what spare ribs existed were needed to make the first woman.

So people ate apples and got knowledge and knew they were missing out on something.

The Prophets: They were sent to make way and prepare the world for Barbecue. They taught the people to set aside vast stores of hickory.

Also, they instructed the people not to worship false foods – like pressed chicken nuggets and tofu.

And there was one – Johnny, the Southern Baptist – who spread the word with a bumper sticker. "Put Some South in Your Mouth," it said.

The Birth: Lo, there were shepherds in the field and they did hear loud sounds from the heavens.

And, looking up, they did not see anything, because what they'd heard was their stomachs growling and echoing over the firmament because they were really hungry.

And they did look to the south where they saw smoke. And drawing closer they saw a fire. Across that fire was a grill and on that grill were some ribs, and they were sizzling mightily and needed turning before they got too crispy on the outside.

Pork ribs. Several humongous slabs of them.

And the shepherds did flip them. And then they did fall on their knees and give praise because, being shepherds, all they had eaten up to that time was mutton. And they were sick of it, sick unto the very death.

There came also, bearing gifts for the Barbecue, the Three Fat Men – Bubba, Jim Bob and Sonny.

Bubba brought the Holy Homemade Sauce.

Jim Bob brought toothpicks.

Sonny brought plenty of extra napkins.

Luckily, the shepherds had lots of beer. And some coleslaw. Also, baked beans.

So they did eat. And eat. And eat some more. After which they watched a ballgame and fell asleep.

And when they had awakened all did agree that Barbecue did hold for them the keys to heaven. So they had the leftovers for dinner. Someone went out and got a watermelon.

Barbecue martyrs: The land was ruled in those days by Romans and there went out a decree that everyone should eat pizza.

Those who refused were rounded up and sent to the Coliseum where they were made to face the lions.

Although it was not as tasty as pork, all the martyrs agreed that barbecued lion was better than no barbecue at all.

Modern schisms: Mostly these have centered on whether the pork should be shredded or sliced and whether the sauce should be sweet and thick with tomato, or sour and thin and vinegary. Barbecue, being an accommodating religion, has room for all beliefs.

Thanks for your kind attention and reverence while we reviewed the Barbecue Story. Now ... go forth and pig out.

Me to the Rescue

I WAS HEADING DOWN THE homestretch, returning from an out-of-town trip, when I stopped at the convenience store. It sat by itself on the highway, nothing else around for a good mile or so.

I don't need much of an excuse to drink beer. Going home after a long day on the road seems about as good a reason as any. So I pulled a six-pack from the cooler and walked up to the counter to pay.

The clerk, short and blonde and in her early 20s, said, "If you don't mind, I'm going to take a long time ringing you up."

"Excuse me?" I said.

"I think there's two guys out there who might be up to something and I don't want to be here alone," she said, pointing out to the gasoline pumps.

They were motorcycle guys. Both were huge, with full beards and lots of hair. They were dressed in standard motorcycle-guy regalia – black leather jackets with the sleeves cut off, black T-shirts, jeans and black boots. They had tattoos, chain belts and wristbands with metal studs. One wore a red bandanna on his head. The other one actually was wearing an eye patch, a black eye patch.

"Friends of yours?" I asked the clerk.

"Yeah, sure," she laughed. "They've been standing out there for 10 or 15 minutes, talking to each other and looking in here. I think they've been waiting until I'm alone so they can pull something."

I gave her my best John Wayne: "So you want me to stick around, ma'am?"

"Uh-huh," she said.

I slid my six-pack to the side, grabbed a sleazy tabloid and pretended to read it, real casual-like. But we all know the track record for violent crime and convenience stores. Not even those sleazy tabloid headlines could grab my attention from what was unfolding around me.

"One of them has a knife," said the clerk.

It was Eye Patch. The knife was in his back pocket. It was a big, bulky thing with a horn handle. It only looked about 10 times as large as the puny Swiss Army knife in my pocket.

"And I'm pretty sure the other one has a gun," said the clerk. "In his front pocket."

Sure enough, there was a bulge that looked like a gun in Red Bandanna's pocket. I looked behind the counter.

"Do you have . . . ?"

"No, I haven't got a gun or nothing," said the clerk. "I've got some hair spray. I read where you can spray that and it will blind someone for a little bit."

I pictured the scene: two big motorcycle guys with knives and guns and us trying to fight them off with a can of Clairol Ultra-Hold. Right. Maybe I could roll up the sleazy tabloid and swat them with it.

"Why don't you call someone," I said.

"Like the cops?" she asked.

"Exactly like the cops," I said.

She was heading for the phone when Red Bandanna walked in the door. The clerk froze. I froze. Outside, I could see Eye Patch cranking up his motorcycle. And I understood how it was going to go down: Red Bandanna would do the dirty work while Eye Patch took care of anyone who pulled up.

I reached for the six-pack of beer. I figured, if nothing else, I could throw it at Red Bandanna and then maybe tackle him or something.

Red Bandanna went for his pocket. But instead of a gun he pulled out two big, greasy bolts and a couple of wing nuts. He stuck them toward the clerk.

"You don't sell anything like this, do you?" he asked.

She gulped and said: "No, but there's a hardware store about 2 miles up the road."

"Thanks," he said, smiling, and walked out the door toward his motorcycle.

He said a few words to Eye Patch, pointing down the road. And then – I kid you not – he reached over, put his arms around Eye

Patch and kissed him. Right on the mouth. They hugged each other and then drove off, side by side.

"I don't believe it," I said.

The clerk didn't say anything, just stood there with her mouth open.

"I'll be damned," she finally said. "I'll just be damned."

"Guess I'll be moseying off now, ma'am," I said, swaggering out the door, heading into the sunset.

I was all the way home before I remembered I had left that six-pack sitting on the counter.

Support in a Nutshell

LIKE ANY LOVING, CONSCIENtious father I strive to make sure my children have it better than I ever had it. A better education. A better exposure to culture and the fine arts. And, of course, a better experience than I had when buying my first jock strap.

(Caution: If at this point you think you might be offended by what is commonly known as "locker-room humor," that is, gratuitous jokes about body parts, crude references to bodily functions or sophomoric remarks about so-called "mature" topics, then I would urge you: Don't be such a wonk.)

Now, where was I? Oh yeah ... a gratuitous joke about body parts.

There was this old Hindu butcher who had a shop in the Hindu part of town, right? The old butcher had an ancient meat scale that he liked very much, but which had long since passed the point where it could be calibrated. And it always underweighed by about a quarter-pound on the pound. So the old Hindu butcher had become adept at applying just enough pressure with a thumb to ensure an accurate reading. He was very discreet about it, since the customers would, of course, think he was cheating them.

Unfortunately, the old butcher was no longer able to haul around heavy sides of beef and had just hired a young assistant, who was running the counter while the butcher took a phone call. Just then, who should walk in but the neighborhood's most prominent Swami, a very good customer, who, despite being Hindu, was exceptionally fond of beef liver. And he asked for 100 pounds of it for a big party he was having.

The old butcher, overhearing the order, was aghast. Why, he'd forgotten to tell the young assistant about the scale's deficiency.

And, on a sale of that magnitude, the butcher stood to lose several dollars, which he could ill-afford.

So, in his rich, sonorous baritone, the butcher sang out: "Weigh down upon the Swami's liver ... "

Okay, okay. So it was a gratuitous joke about a COW body part. At least it poked fun at the Official State Song of Florida, which is one thing that just can't be done often enough. And, having suffered through it, I'd think you'd actually welcome a discussion of jock straps.

I did not buy my first one until I was in the seventh grade at Leesburg High School. It was the first day of the school year and when it came time for P.E. Coach Bud "Bud" Headlock, who would later lecture us for nearly an hour on the various ways in which one can get a hernia, sat us all down and said: "Young men. Jock straps."

And we all sat there extremely puzzled, wondering: "What is Coach Bud trying to tell us? That we ARE jock straps? What have we ever done to him, anyway?"

What Coach Bud meant, of course, was that since we were seventh graders and had therefore spontaneously and against our wills become young men we were required to wear jock straps whenever we dressed out for gym. That, of course, meant going out and buying one. Because it wasn't like you could borrow one.

"And for convenience and a reasonable price – plus, to help out your school – I'd strongly suggest buying your jock straps and anything else you might need at the athletic department store, which is located right out there in the hall," Coach Bud said.

The next day, before gym class, several of us went to the athletic department store. And there, to our unspeakable horror, we discovered that the person behind the counter was not one of the coaches, but Mary Fuhrbringer, head majorette, senior class goddess and the object of certain fantasies that shall not be discussed here.

We seventh grade boys, flush with the first rages of puberty, were supposed to buy our jock straps from her?

We all walked up to the counter together. Someone nudged Eddie Lieberman forward. And Eddie cleared his throat and managed to say, "One jock strap, please," just as coolly as if he'd been ordering a double cheeseburger.

Mary Sue was very bored by it all. She could not even begin to fathom the excruciating agony of the moment. She just looked at Eddie and said: "What size?"

What size? What size? What did she mean what size? How did you measure?

What did you measure?

"Uh, uh . . . small, I guess," Eddie said. And while the rest of us snickered at all that implied – guys are just like that – Mary retrieved Eddie's order and took his money. Then she looked at me.

"Same thing," I said.

"Small?" asked Mary.

I do not know what got into me. New hormones. Being 13 years old. Wanting to show off in front of my buddies.

"Unh-uh," I said. "Extra large."

And I was feeling pretty cool and all the guys were getting a big laugh when Mary Fuhrbringer snorted and said: "You mean . . . an extra large peanut shell and a rubber band, don't you?"

It was a great comeback, I'll give her that, and the first time any of us had ever heard that line. Only I wish it hadn't been me playing Mary's straight man.

It got all over the school. Next day I showed up for P.E. and Coach Bud said: "Hey, Morris! Remember your peanut shell?"

That's why I wanted my sons to have a better experience when it came time for buying their first jock straps, which happened not long ago under instructions from their Little League coach.

On the way to the sporting goods store I gave them a little talk about the importance of wearing proper protective devices when playing sports. I sounded a lot like Coach Bud, I'm afraid.

I told them that while jock straps were personal undergarments, there was no reason to be embarrassed about buying one. And I told them about the first time I bought one, including Mary Fuhrbringer's memorable remark. They got a big laugh.

We picked out two jock straps. We got in the checkout line. I knew the guy at the cash register. He picked up one of the cartons and, winking, said to me: "Wear a size 'Small,' do you?"

And we both chuckled. Because guys are like that.

And that's when my son Dash announced for the benefit of all: "No, he doesn't. My daddy wears a peanut shell and a rubber band!"

The kids cracked up. The guy at the cash register cracked up. But I don't think the nice lady standing behind us with the two little girls approved.

No, I don't think she approved at all.

And Mary Fuhrbringer, wherever you are, gee, have a nice day.

Rolling for Rolexes

••••••••••••••••••••

WHY YES, THAT IS A ROLEX YOU see on my wrist. It is a ridiculously expensive watch. I hope you realize that. You darn well better realize that.

When you look at my Rolex you are supposed to think: "I am in the presence of a human being for whom it is nothing to spend thousands of dollars just to know what time of day it is."

Of course, some of you might also think: "I believe I'll roll this sucker, steal his watch, hock it and buy something that makes sense."

That is, after all, what owning a Rolex is about. It creates a distinct impression. Need I say more?

Well, yes, I do need to say more, actually, since this column requires another 700 words and since I didn't pay thousands of dollars for this Rolex. If I had thousands of dollars just lying around I would not spend it on some pretentious wristwatch. If I had even $9.95 just lying around – which in my case is just as likely as the thousands – I would not spend it on some cheapo digital wristwatch either, not even if it was one of those cheapo digital wristwatches that also doubles as a powerful calculator and that could serenade me at the top of every hour with "Roll Out the Barrel."

Let me tell you my idea of the perfect time-keeping device – the sundial.

The sundial was invented by the ancient Egyptians, generally regarded as the smartest people who ever lived. The Egyptians were so smart that they could have gone ahead and invented Rolexes and cheapo digital wristwatches if they had wanted to, but they didn't. They realized that, with sundials, life was ideal. And it was ideal because most of the time we have so much trouble keeping up with these days just didn't exist.

For instance, there was no such thing as 4:32 p.m., just to pick one of my least favorite times of day, since it means this column is supposed to be finished in 28 minutes and I am only just here. With sundials it was either "about 4" or "about 5." The ancient Egyptians were pretty loose about that. Looser than my editors.

Plus, you know how it has been raining for two days solid and we haven't even seen the sun? Well, if this had taken place in ancient Egypt, you wouldn't have been able to tell what time it was. So whenever it rained, time in ancient Egypt was temporarily suspended, which meant you didn't have to go to work. You could just lounge around the shack reading hieroglyphics. Also, time never existed after the sun set. So, late at night, there was never a need for the bars to have last call. They just stayed open. I think we can all agree that life during sundials was far superior. But it explains why it took thousands of years to build those pyramids.

Still, this doesn't explain why I am wearing a Rolex, does it? I am wearing a Rolex because of my father-in-law. He died a couple of years ago and left me his Rolex. He did this for two reasons: (1) he loved me, and (2) he was aware of my aversion to wristwatches and knew that owning an expensive, pretentious one would really bug me. This is sometimes what you do to people you love.

So every now and then I wear the Rolex. And automatically it's as if I belong to this club that I don't have any business belonging to. You get noticed by other Rolex wearers. It is the strangest thing.

I've had grown men stop me on the street and say, "How do you like that model?" as if I were wearing an automobile on my arm. Then they feel compelled to show me their models and discuss the wonderfulness of keeping precise track of time. I don't do a very good job holding up my end of the conversation.

Other times I've had them wink or nod meaningfully in such a way that, to tell you the truth, I was alarmed as to their intentions, until I realized that they merely wanted to give notice we were both wearing the same model Rolex. Ah, male bonding.

And once, in the grocery checkout line, this guy handed me his card and said: "When you are interested in trading up, give me a call." Trading up what? My house? I must have looked confused because he pointed at my watch. "I sell those," he said. Then he pointed at his watch. And he actually said: "Ten thousand dollars –

it's the diamonds."

It looked nice. I was very impressed. It was everything I could do not to roll the sucker, steal the thing, hock it and buy something that makes sense.

Where the Money Goes

THE KID FROM DOWN the street strolls into our house. On his way to meet my sons in their bedroom, he stops by the sliding glass doors that lead to our back yard. He says:

"Hey, lookit! You've got a green pool! I mean, it is really green. Don't you ever clean it or nothing? I haven't ever seen a pool that green before. It's the greenest pool I ..."

The kid is pretty fast on his feet, so he is gone by the time I take a swat at him. But I look for myself and, sure enough, the pool is green. It looks like a 26,000-gallon vat of lime Kool-Aid.

Which is amazing because that very morning, like every morning, I was poolside with my handy-dandy All-In-One Pool Test Kit, playing Mr. Wizard. I should mention that the only reason I am in the column-writing business is that I wanted to be a marine biologist but flunked college chemistry three times. So understand that it is a major accomplishment for me to take daily water samples and perform the chemistry tests necessary to make my pool appear as pure as a baptismal font.

But I do it. Because I am a Floridian. By law I must maintain a pool. And that very morning, the chlorine was right, the pH was balanced, the pool was perfect.

What happened in the meantime was what happens every meantime in Florida during the summer: It rained. It rained a lot. And whenever it rains the pool turns green.

"It's a rain-borne algae that makes it do that," says Bob, my man at the pool supply store where I no longer consider myself a customer but a sustaining member. Bob hands me an 8-ounce canister of powdered algicide that sells for $10. That makes a total of $249,376 I've spent on pool chemicals this summer.

When it comes time for my kids to go to college, I am going to give them some Mason jars, point them toward the pool and say: "Go forth, sell that water and pay for your tuition. I have invested heavily in it. It is now worth $7,000 a half-pint."

People ask me what I do on weekends. I tell them I go diving. What I don't tell them is that I go diving with a steel brush in one hand and a stick of chlorine in the other hand, doing combat with the algae that is thriving in my green pool.

And do not look closely at my clothes. My only pair of dress shoes are not wingtips. But they have that nifty wingtip pattern of little holes because I forgot to remove them when I was giving the pool its dose of muriatic acid. Also, I am prepared to be in vogue whenever fashion dictates a casual wardrobe of shorts with chlorine splotches.

Pool owners I talk to say they are going nuts trying to keep their pools from looking like sludge ponds. They say this summer has been worse than any other summer. And I have a theory on the reason:

Canada.

You know how Canada has been complaining about the factories in the United States being responsible for all the acid rain that is falling on that country?

Well, Canada is getting even. The Canadian border is now lined with massive algae factories. After our acid rain clouds dump on Canada, the Canadians shoot the clouds full of algae and send them back south. The result is people like me spending a fourth of our discretionary income and most weekends making sure we don't contract cholera, the Plague, creeping eruption and whatever else you can catch from an unhealthy swimming pool.

And I bet if you looked into it, you would find that Canadians own all the swimming pool supply stores. I can tell by the way Bob chuckles whenever I walk in. He and his cohorts get pleasure out of my pool problems.

So I've stopped doing business with them. And I have contracted with the federal government, which is making me a great deal on some leftover defoliants and herbicides that once were used to denude the landscape in Southeast Asia. Because what we're talking about here is war.

And soon, my pool will be blue. It will be that shade of blue that can be achieved only if you make it impossible for the water to support any form of life whatsoever. Innocent toads will jump in and disintegrate. Wandering dogs will drink from my pool and howl. I will call up the kid from down the street, invite him for a swim and ... heh-heh.

The Call of the Game

••••••••••••••••••

MY MOST LUCID MEMORY OF A FRIDAY night in the fall finds me standing in the back yard of the house where I grew up. It is about 7 p.m., an hour before kickoff. I am 12 years old and impatient in the manner of an older brother who is forced to wait on two younger brothers and a sister. The stadium is less than a mile away, and I am ready to be there.

Actually, stadium is an aggrandizement of terms; it was just some rickety bleachers that kids could fall through, often did. And the playing field, despite the best efforts of coaches who regularly had the boys' physical education classes move irrigation pipes, was little more than wiregrass and dust. But it had bright lights atop tall creosote poles, and on Friday nights in the fall, Leesburg (smallish then in the way that all Central Florida towns once were) had nothing else that could compete. Not even fans of the visiting team who lacked all sense of direction could fail to find the stadium. The sky above it was that bright.

And so I stood in the back yard, looking toward the lights. It was probably that first night of the fall when a new pair of jeans stops being prickly hot and feels comfortable. It was probably the night my mom had made the season's first pot of chili. The air was not quite crisp but as close as it comes to crisp that time of year in Florida. And cutting through it, above the sound of semis on U.S. Highway 27, was the steady thump-thumping of a big, bass drum.

I could picture that drum, taller even than the boy who beat it, the Leesburg High School Yellow Jacket emblem stenciled on each side. But most of all I could feel it. It was insistent – a call to assemble that could not be ignored. I had never before, and rarely have since, felt so drawn to a place as I felt drawn to that Friday night football game.

Surely those who have grown up in the city have felt something similar. Friday night football games are played most everywhere. But they take on added significance in small towns. Municipal fervor is drastically diluted in a city where its several high schools bear names of things vaguely geographic (Oak Ridge, Edgewater) or departed public servants (William R. Boone, Maynard Evans). In a small town where the name of the town is the name of the school, the Friday night brew tends to be full strength. It is not merely school against school, but town against town. Witness historic rivalries like Eustis vs. Mount Dora, Groveland vs. Clermont, Leesburg vs. Wildwood.

You could argue that pro football, with its big city franchises, is more capable of distilling metropolitan zeal. But you would be arguing wrong. Sure the Giants can draw 60,000, but that is in a city of 12 million. Compare that with Dunnellon, the Marion County town where I lived before moving to Orlando. Fewer than 1,000 registered voters there, but you could count on three times that number when Dunnellon played Crystal River.

You get life's rich assortment at a Friday night high school game. You get mamas and daddies selling peanuts so the band can have new uniforms. You get little girls lined up against the fence mimicking the cheerleaders. You get the announcer at halftime saying: "Would all the members of the Class of 1977 reunion please stand up and wave to the press box so we can get you on videotape?" You get to see whose daughter is going out with whose son. You get all the local politicos taking time to work the crowd. You get the future stars of the gridiron playing a pick-up game beneath the stands. You get the heart and soul of a town. And it cannot help but do your own heart and soul some good.

Which is why I require regular doses of Friday night games in small towns.

Another memory comes to mind: I am just out of college, working for the newspaper in Fort Myers, far away from friends and family. A certain amount of loneliness has set in. I hit the road on Friday night, trying to drive it all out, when I see that far-off glow in the sky. There is nothing else to do. I just keep heading for it. I wind up in La Belle. I find the stadium. La Belle is playing Clewiston.

I get out of my car, and the first thing I hear is that bass drum. (Did I mention before that the pounding is like a heartbeat?) Suddenly all is right with the world.

Middleword
for
Bob's Book
by
Dave Barry

At this point you've read a bunch of Bob Morris' columns, and you probably have some questions about him, such as:

1. He gets *paid* to write this stuff?
2. With actual *money?*
3. How can I get a job like that?

Believe me, Bob's job is not as easy as it seems. Like him, I am also a highly trained professional journalist, and I know that the columns you see here are only the *end product* of Bob's efforts. Before he writes a column, he puts in countless hours of hard work doing intensive research, even if this requires him to stay up late and drink a whole lot of beer.

This is what he was doing when I met him. This was in 1988, when we were both in Iowa to cover the presidential caucuses. There were a lot of journalists there, most of them responsible, serious, suit-wearing people, indistinguishable from accountants, who tended to sit around earnestly discussing the issues. But not Bob. The night I met him, in a Des Moines bar, he was talking about the birthplace of John Wayne, which he had visited that day while all the other journalists were out taking Michael Dukakis seriously. Also Bob was very excited about the fact that he had found a restaurant that appeared to be located in a concrete factory. This is the essence of Bob: Whatever serious, responsible journalists are doing, he is doing something else.

Since that night, it has been my honor to cover a number of major news stories with Bob, and I'm pleased to report that in all the time we've spent together, we have never, not once, discussed the issues. This is not to say that we've been idle. We have committed a number of important acts of journalism. For example, in 1988, at the

Democratic National Convention in Atlanta, Bob and I and a *Seattle Times* columnist named Erik Lacitis conducted a scientific experiment to prove our theory that the amount of media coverage an event gets is directly proportional to how stupid the event is.

The way we did this was, we went to the official area that the Democrats had established for holding protests in, and we put cardboard boxes over our heads. Then we just stood there, waiting, three guys with boxes on our heads.

We didn't have to wait long. Within minutes we were surrounded by reporters, TV camera crews, photographers and radio people, thrusting cameras and microphones at us and asking us questions.

We were very honest with them.

They'd say: "Who are you?"

We'd say: "We're people with boxes over our heads."

They'd say: "What are you doing?"

We'd say: "We're standing here with boxes over our heads."

The next day we were a national news story. Pictures of the Boxhead Protest appeared in newspapers from coast to coast. When we revealed our secret identities, a lot of serious journalists were *very* ticked off at us for Making a Mockery out of the press. You can imagine how we felt.

Later that summer the national media descended on New Orleans for the Republican convention, a week of gradually increasing dramatic tension, building toward the big moment when George Bush would accept the presidential nomination. Every serious news person wanted to see this in person, so Bob and I decided that there was only one place we could be when it happened: the motel room where Jimmy Swaggart got caught with a prostitute. And so that's where we went. We had to bribe our way in, but it was worth it, because the room had a special TV set with a switch on the side; if you flicked it up, you saw George Bush accepting the nomination, and if you flicked it down, you saw two people engaging in acts of unusually closer friendship. It was the best acceptance speech I ever saw tiny snippets of.

I could go on and on, giving true anecdotes to illustrate the many ways in which Bob has advanced the frontiers of journalism. But this is his book, and I don't want to take up too much space. My main point is that a lot of behind-the-scenes work has gone into the columns you're reading here.

It's a tough job, being Bob Morris, and you should be proud of the fact that you have contributed to his welfare by purchasing this book. In fact, now that you're aware of the sacrifices he has made, you might even want to give Bob a cash donation. Just send it to me, and I'll make sure he gets it. You can trust me. I'm a journalist.

Needing the Fair

●●●●●●●●●●●●●●●●●●●●●●

I LOOK AT THE PIG WITH Human Hands and Human Feet. And the Pig with Human Hands and Human Feet looks back at me.

Or at least the Pig with Human Hands and Human Feet would look back at me if the Pig with Human Hands and Human Feet were alive. It is not. It is dead and in a jar alongside other dead things in jars like the Cyclops Pig and the Two-Headed Rabbit and the Devil's Child – "one of the world's most curios (sic) freaks, this was found on city dump of Utica, N.Y."

It wasn't supposed to be like this. It wasn't supposed to be like this at all. Outside, the posters and banners that lured me in promise an altogether different scene. They show the Cyclops Pig and the Two-Headed Rabbit at full gallop, terrorizing standard breed barnyard critters. The Devil's Child has fire in his eyes as he carries out some black magic treachery. And the Pig with Human Hands and Human Feet? The Pig with Human Hands and Human Feet is stretched out in a hammock, pretty as you please, sipping at a glass of lemonade and looking every bit as big as you or me.

But inside, after the ticket is bought, that pickled pig in a jar ain't but 3 inches long, maybe 4. You can't even tell if it has really got human hands and human feet. And for one brief moment I consider marching out to the ticket taker, telling him the whole thing's a fake and demanding my $1.40 back.

Then perspective returns. Sure, I've been had. So what? This is, after all, the fair, the Central Florida Fair. And at the fair, at any fair anywhere, everything – the whole wretched, wonderful mess – is fair.

We're all fair game. We know the rules. We know what to expect before we arrive, which is why we keep returning to the fair year after year.

We know that winning a kewpie doll in the ring toss is unlikely. We know that Bobo the Dunk-A-Clown insults us just to get our money. And we know that the Pig with Human Hands and Human Feet isn't all it's made out to be.

That's the fair's appeal. It has bluster. It has guts. It teases. It taunts. And it dares us to come back for more.

By all rights, Central Florida should be one tough market for a fair. Consider the competition. We have been spoiled by state-of-the-art theme parks that glisten and shine, where everything is aboveboard, where squeaky-clean attendants never insult us and where there is just no place for tawdry elements like the Pig with Human Hands and Human Feet. How can a fair, an ordinary fair, possibly hold its own against that?

Still, they are predicting 300,000 of us will traipse out to the Central Florida Fairgrounds before the show packs up and leaves town. For all our so-called sophistication, there is plenty of bumpkin that remains in our souls.

We need the fair. After all the wonder of our Living Seas and our killer whale shows, we need such down-to-earth superlatives as "The Smallest Horse in the World" (15 inches long, 6 pounds at birth) or "Florida's Largest Alligator" (13 feet long, 1,000 pounds). We need to drop a quarter to see the "Drumming Duck" or the "Basketball Playing Chicken" or the "Kissing Bunny."

Forget all our fancy restaurants. We need an evening when Polish sausage and Texas-style onion rings meet all our culinary expectations.

High-tech gizmos and computers are everywhere we turn. Once in a while we need to savor some down-home arts and crafts displays. We need to see for ourselves that a red pinwheel design won this year's blue ribbon for "Best Quilt," that Carol S. Richardson took best of show for "Best Decorated Cake" and Cindi Meriwether walked off with top honors in "Yeast Baking, Junior Division."

We need to wander through the 4-H stalls, amidst the rich aroma of Santa Gertrudis, Polled Herefords and Black Angus. It even does our bumpkin souls good to get cow flop on our shoes.

I tell the Pig with Human Hands and Human Feet goodbye. Goodbye until next year.

Outside, a little boy is pleading with his mom. "Aw, c'mon, please," he says. "I want to go see that pig."

I look at his mom and say: "It's really great. Let him go."

Everyone needs to see that pig. Everyone needs the fair.

A Florida Century

FOR THE OFFICIAL JAMES FAMILY portrait, John and Ellen James – he in a white linen suit, she in a high-collared dress – sat in rocking chairs surrounded by their five children.

The daughters – May and Daisy – wore long, white gowns drawn tight at the waist. They had good figures. The two younger sons – Roland and Stanley – sported dark, wool suits that were too short in the arms. They must have itched like crazy. Ray, the oldest son, with his work shirt hanging half out and his straw hat askew, looked like he came straight from the fields.

None of them smiled.

Years later, some of their smart-alecky progeny, I among them, would look at the James family portrait, its background a wild and impenetrable cabbage palm jungle, and laughingly dub it "Lost in the Everglades."

The James family wasn't really lost. And the setting wasn't really the Everglades. It was Yalaha, Lake County, Florida, circa 1903, not quite 20 years after the James family left England for a new home.

The James family wasn't really the James family either. But that was a well-kept secret, one that didn't surface until my grandmother, May, the firstborn child and the last of the original family, was on her deathbed in 1973.

"Our last name is really Booth," she told us. "We changed it when we left England."

My grandmother offered no explanations. Birth records in England subsequently showed the family name was, indeed, Booth.

Did they drop it because another Booth – John Wilkes – had a few years earlier assassinated the president of their newly claimed country? Or was their reason more ordinary – to escape creditors perhaps?

Every family needs its mystery, I suppose. That's ours. And that's just one of the things we talked about Saturday at the James family reunion to honor the 100th anniversary of our forebears' arrival in Florida.

Judged by standards elsewhere – certain New Englanders can proudly trace their lineage back to the Pilgrims and 1620 – 100 years is but a blink. This is Florida though, where some counties have Pioneer Clubs that require a mere 50-year legacy for membership, where 25-year residents can be considered elder statesmen, where even 10 years can win you longtimer's status.

So 100 years is a handsome chunk of time on this spit of land where, back in 1886 my great-grandfather James started the business – he was the first fern grower in Florida – that's run now by my father and brother.

There are no Jameses left, by surname at least. None of the James brothers had sons. But from the original seven in that "Lost in the Everglades" portrait, we number now 125, most living in Central Florida. And 70 of us showed up to celebrate our centennial here.

We don't get together often. Like all families, some of us have had our feuds and have gone for years without speaking. In fact, this was the first time within anyone's memory that the entire family had been called together. There were some who had never seen each other before.

We met at a park in Leesburg, as varied an assortment of folks as you can imagine. Doctors and farmers, shopkeepers and teachers, some who have done a little bit of everything and some who haven't done much at all. There were some who have moved to the big cities and others who still live in the houses where they were born more than 60 years ago. There were lots of little kids running around and raising Cain. No one complained.

We played horseshoes (my cousin Bill and I claimed the championship). Cousin Turnley played the guitar. We all played the "Do you remember when . . . ?" game. There was lots of picture-taking and lots of hugging and lots of looking at the old sepia photographs that are our treasured link to those who came before us. We all wore little name tags bearing a copy of that "Lost in the Everglades" portrait.

When it came time to give the blessing, the Episcopalian beer drinkers donated an ice chest for the Church of God preacher to use as a pulpit. He kept it short. He said all those who came before us were with us there that day.

I'm pretty sure he was right.

And I'm pretty sure they were smiling.

Take a Powder

●●●●●●●●●●●●●●●●●●●●●

I HAD A HEADACHE. IT WAS NOT one of those headaches you can just ignore and it will go away.

I think this particular headache was caused by all the pollen in the air lately. Used to be pollen didn't bother me. But when I turned 40, things changed. Pollen started clogging me up. I tried to figure out exactly why this should be. It only made my headache worse.

I went to the medicine cabinet. Nothing there but children's Tylenol. I considered chewing the six grape-flavored tablets that remained. The tiny print on the side of the bottle said six tablets were the recommended dosage for a 90-pound child. I weigh considerably more than 90 pounds. Just how much more is one of those things that makes my head ache. So does reading tiny print without my glasses.

I got in my car and drove to the closest convenience store. It was bright outside. I forgot my sunglasses. My headache reached the point where I could have swallowed the recommended dosage of children's Tylenol for a 736-pound kid and it wouldn't have made any difference.

I got out of my car at the convenience store and walked toward the door. I hate people who spit out chewing gum where other people can step in it, don't you?

As I was scraping the gum off my shoe a helpful man walked by and said: "If you stick an ice cube on that it will come off a lot easier." I hate people who spit out unsolicited advice to people with headaches.

There were lots of headache remedies on the shelves at the convenience store. Didn't make any difference to me. I knew what I wanted. I wanted B.C. headache powder. Nothing else would possibly do.

I don't care if this sounds like an advertisement. B.C. headache powder is my choice for headache relief. The reason I like B.C. is that it doesn't come in a tablet or a capsule. They just give you the powder straight, all ground up and loose inside a folded-over piece of waxed paper. Seems like that makes it work faster.

Also, you pour B.C. headache powder into your mouth and it tastes something awful. It tastes so awful that it immediately makes you forget your headache. All you want to do is wash your mouth out. So I got a soft drink.

There were three clerks at the counter and suddenly I was a 40-year-old man with a headache who was invisible. Finally, they consented to let me pay.

I went out to my car. It is a convertible. The top was down and the wind was blowing. I opened the wax paper with the powder in it and poured it in the direction of my mouth. I missed. The powder went all over my beard.

I cussed. Loudly. So loudly that the woman with the three children who was getting out of the minivan next to me turned around and gave me one of those looks I'd give someone who cussed loudly in front of my children.

"Sorry," I said, wiping the headache powder off my beard.

The woman gave me a hard, hard look. She pulled her children toward her and hurried inside the store.

I got out another headache powder. This time it was on target. I sipped some of the soft drink. I had a newspaper sitting in the car and glanced at the sports page because I had missed it that morning. I got involved with a story.

Then I decided to take another powder. And sip some more of the drink. And finish reading the story. I was feeling better.

Then a police car pulled in, blocking me, just as I was getting ready to crank up and leave.

"Don't move," said the officer. "Stay right there."

I didn't budge.

"Now get out slowly." He was sweating a lot. He looked like he might have a headache, too. He wasn't particularly gentle when he patted me down.

"Mind if I look inside your vehicle?" he asked, already looking. He picked up the packet of B.C. headache powder.

"You just take some of this?" he asked.

"Sure did," I told him.

He held it up and waved it at the woman with the three children who was watching the scene from inside the store with the three clerks.

"They called," the officer said. "They thought you were taking something else."

The officer said I could go home.

"Have a nice day," he actually said.

When I got home I read the tiny print on the back of the B.C. headache powder packet. It said wait at least two hours between doses. I didn't.

Coffee With Extra Prayers

●●●●●●●●●●●●●●●●●●●●●●

IT WAS JUST ANOTHER HIGHWAY restaurant, a place outside of Tampa where they served decent biscuits and tolerable coffee. Plus, they didn't seem to care how long you occupied space in one of the padded vinyl booths. I appreciated that. My car had broken down, and I needed somewhere to sit and stew while the mechanic put together his damage report.

I had read everything the paper had to offer. I had poured yet another cup of coffee. And I was doing what I like to do best when circumstances force me to sit alone in a restaurant. I was eavesdropping.

Off to one side a couple of waitresses were talking about their tips, their horoscopes and their troubles.

The people behind me, a man and two women, must have all worked in the same office. They were laying out the details about who was running around with whom.

And then there were the two men sitting in the booth in front of me. They looked to be in their 50s. One had slicked-back silver hair and wore a business suit. On his lapel was a plastic nameplate with a real estate company logo. His name was Warren.

The other fellow had the look of a man who has spent many years working outside. A citrus grower maybe, or a cattle rancher. He had on a khaki shirt, and his khaki pants were tucked into his boots. There were sun splotches all over his face.

They had pushed aside their breakfast plates, and each had pulled out a book. Both books had worn, nondescript covers with all sorts of markers and papers stuck between the pages. I figured they were ledgers or sales records and that the men were fixing to talk business.

But then Warren said: "Brother Peterson, I'd like us to read Psalm 62."

So they flipped the pages of their well-thumbed Bibles until they found it. Warren began. Later, I had to look up that Psalm to get all the words straight, but what he read was: "Truly my soul waiteth upon God: from Him cometh my salvation."

Brother Peterson took the second verse. In a soft drawl, not much more than a whisper, he said: "He only is my rock and salvation; He is my defense; I shall not be greatly moved."

And in this way, each taking a verse, Warren and Brother Peterson finished Psalm 62.

I am not a man without faith, but neither am I one to sit in a restaurant reading the Psalms out loud. It's just not my way, nor is it the way of the church in which I was brought up.

Generally, I'm put off by those who display their faith too flagrantly, who try to foist their religion on others, damning any who would dare differ. Like some of those TV preachers. You know the ones. Through all their electronic hype they sometimes make us forget there are still plenty of pastors content to mind small congregations and tend to the spiritual needs of their flock, without the trappings of expensive suits, fancy cars and grand houses, pastors who don't mind taking the time to visit you when you're sick, comfort you when you're distressed or just chat over a cup of coffee from time to time.

And that's just the kind of pastor that Warren and Mr. Peterson were looking for. From what I could gather of their conversation, the preacher at their church had decided to move on. They were in charge of finding a replacement and were meeting to discuss just what kind of a preacher they wanted.

So I sat there and listened to them talk it over. They talked a lot about their families. They talked a lot about their faith. They talked about, as Warren said, the importance of finding "someone who will lead with love and teach with love."

Yeah, I know. It sounds pretty corny. And it's easy to be cynical when you hear people talking this way. But there was something about listening to these two men talk – and talk from their hearts – that made me feel good.

"Brother Peterson, would you say a prayer before we go?" asked Warren.

Both men bowed their heads and closed their eyes. Brother Peterson kept it short. He asked for guidance. He asked for strength. And he asked for the courage to persevere even when things look bad.

"Amen," they both said. Then they got up and left.

Amen, indeed. And may their prayers be answered.

Perfect World

THIS IS NOT A PERFECT WORLD. That is why I am in need.

I am in need of a few good people to establish a few much-needed professions. I would hire them to do certain things that I simply cannot do. I would pay them well. So would others like me. We would all be happy. The world would be a better place.

Just how much we need these new professions is demonstrated in the following case studies that I only wish I could say were not taken from real life:

The sod man arrives early in the morning to give me a new lawn. He's a nice guy. We get along, exchanging small talk, buddy-buddy. I like to get along with people. This is a major character flaw.

One of the sod man's workers is operating a big, noisy machine that chews up my old lawn.

"Is that thing going to eat my sprinkler system?" I ask the sod man.

"Just mark your sprinkler heads and it will be all right," he says.

So I mark the sprinkler heads with tiny orange flags the sod man gives me. Then the sod man and I stand around some more, shooting the shinola, talking sports and the weather. Nice guy.

A few hours later my new lawn is in place. It looks great. I give the sod man a check for $723.46.

"You need to get some water on that lawn right away," the sod man says.

So I turn on the sprinkler system and . . . there's a small geyser in the middle of my new lawn. Then another. And another. I am now the proud owner of an underground fountain system.

"That needs to be fixed," I tell the sod man. Meaning that he should fix it.

"Yeah," he agrees. "It does need to be fixed. Or else you are going to lose that new sod."

"It needs to be fixed right away," I say.

"I wish I knew more about fixing sprinkler systems, I really do," says the sod man, shaking his head, full of sympathy, still buddy-buddy. "There's probably someone you can call in the Yellow Pages."

Then the sod man sticks out his hand. I actually shake it. He drives away.

Nice guy.

And I spend the next day and a half tearing up the new sod, digging in the dirt, replacing PVC pipe, going to the hardware store four times, slicing my thumb with a hacksaw, getting pipe cement all over everything and taking it all out on my wife and kids. Because I like to get along with people. Whenever I can.

If this were a perfect world – and I am convinced that it can be – the moment the sod man stuck out his hand, I would have said: "Wait right there. I need to call my P.I.R."

Then my professional Pain-In-the-Rear would arrive.

"Listen, bub," my P.I.R. would say, "that sprinkler system worked when you got here and it is gonna work before you leave, or else I will see to it that you never do business in this town again.

"Got that? Huh? Do ya?"

My P.I.R. would be cheaper than an attorney.

Quicker, too. And the two of us would shoot the shinola, talk about sports and the weather, while we watched the sod man fixing the sprinklers.

My editor and I sit down to talk. He tells me I am getting a raise. Like always it is not much of a raise. So, also like always, I immediately agree.

If this were a perfect world ...

"Just a moment," I would tell my editor. "I would like you to talk to my Whiner."

Then I would step out of the room while my stand-in Whiner did the job.

"Bob works soooooooooo hard," my Whiner would begin. "Plus, he's got all these bills and he'd like a new boat and a nice vacation and he wants to send his kids to college and he works SOOOOOOOOOOO hard ..."

I do not want to join a union. I do not want an agent. I just want someone to occasionally remind my boss how great I am and grovel a bit and convince my boss that I need a lot more money than I am getting. I would be glad to give my Whiner some of it.

The toilet is leaking. I have tried for weeks to fix it. I have replaced all the innards. Nothing I do works. Finally I call the plumber and, totally exasperated, tell him I need a brand-new toilet. It costs $150. As the plumber is leaving I ask him what was wrong with the old toilet.

"Well, there was this little plastic tube that supplies the water and you had it hooked up outside of the flush pipe instead of inside the flush pipe," he explains.

"That's all?" I ask.

"That's all," he says.

"Well," I say. "Sure is a nice, new toilet."

But better that I should have called my Gramps.

Gramps would be a kindly old gent who knows how to fix everything, but who is more inclined to just sit there and tell you how to fix it – the middleman before you actually need a handyman.

"Why there's your problem right there. Just stick that little tube inside the pipe," Gramps would say. "Don't you know anything?"

Gramps would be entitled to ridicule you. Because he'd only cost half as much as a plumber.

The doorbell rings. It is a Jehovah's Witness. Once when I was in college my roommate bet me that I would not go to the door stark naked when the Jehovah's Witness showed up. I won the bet. Now that I am an adult I can no longer get away with this.

"Have you given any thought to how you'll spend eternity?" the Jehovah's Witness asks when I open the door.

And, like always, I say: "Yes, I have. Now go away." And then I slam the door.

But this really isn't fair to either one of us. The Jehovah's Witnesses should have their say. And, because I have religious opinions of my own, I should have my say.

But who's got the time?

I would call my Mobile Theologian, who would be well-versed in where I stood on the hereafter.

My Mobile Theologian would stand around and discuss religion until the Jehovah's Witness went away. Or until he had to get naked.

If this were a perfect world ...

Postcards from the Past

I AM NOT BY NATURE A collector. When I was a kid, some well-meaning adult gave me a grab bag of 1,000 stamps from all over the world and an album to stick them in. I sat down and looked at each and every stamp. I liked them well enough, but saw no good reason to ever look at them again. None of the stamps ever made it into the album. I have never possessed the fastidiousness it takes to mount a proper collection of anything.

So it was altogether out of character that I began collecting postcards. This was, oh, a dozen years ago. A friend sent me a typical, tacky Florida postcard showing an alligator biting a woman in a bathing suit. It was so awful I taped it to the wall by my desk.

Then someone sent me another one. Different woman, different alligator, just as awful. It went up on the wall, too. Soon I was looking for and actually buying variations on the theme of alligators-biting-women whenever I visited places where tacky postcards were sold. This being Florida, it turned out to be fairly often.

The genre was a bit confining. So I branched out to include alligators-in-general. Then women-in-bathing-suits-in-general. Finally, I found myself accumulating any typical, tacky Florida postcard I could get my hands on.

It was all baffling and out of the blue, this attraction to postcards. There was no explanation for it, at least none that I was aware of at the time.

Little did I know it was in my genes.

By the time I became acquainted with my grandmother Morris – we called her Bama – and her sister, my great-Aunt Daisy, they were both old ladies, grand old ladies, the kind who came heavily powdered, smelling of rose petal sachet and willing to sit for hours listening to anything you had to say.

They've both been dead almost 20 years now. I did not get to know them nearly well enough.

But I have their postcards. There must be 500-600 of them, stuck into two brittle albums that threaten to fall apart at the slightest touch. We came across them a couple of years ago, tucked away in a closet at my parents' house.

Bama and Aunt Daisy were raised in the wilds of Florida after their parents moved from England to Yalaha, in Lake County, back in 1886. There were no telephones, of course. But the mail ran regularly. Picture postcards were just coming into vogue. And the two young women used both to great advantage.

Funny, I had never been able to imagine my grandmother and my great aunt as young women until I sat down with those old postcards. Flipping through the albums, the imagining came easy – about them, about their loves and their lives, about a Florida that used to be ...

"We missed the two of you at the dance last Saturday," reads one postmarked 1903, when Bama would have been 20. The picture shows a steamboat on the Oklawaha River. And the message is from a girlfriend in Leesburg. "The boys all say a dance is not a dance without you girls from Yalaha. But at least I got their attention for a change. Think you can manage to stay home this Saturday, too?"

Another from the same year, written by a friend named Evelyn: "There is to be a dance here tomorrow night and can't you all come over? Someone here is very anxious to see you, but wishes me not to tell you his name."

Which leads us to Mr. E.J. Hamm, a gentleman about whom I know nothing, except that he was one of my Aunt Daisy's many suitors. Apparently, he met her on a trip to Florida and was smitten. The album is filled with dozens of his postcards from the road.

From Asheville, N.C., with the picture of a waterfall: "They say this is the perfect spot for honeymooners. Hmmmm????"

From Knoxville, Tenn., with the picture of two lovers gazing at the moon: "Could this be us?"

From Cleveland: "Why haven't you written? I will be in Chicago next and do expect some brief word."

"Please have pity," reads the postcard from St. Louis. "Just one line from you?"

It's the last card in the album from E.J. Hamm.

When they weren't out dancing and breaking hearts, there were other diversions. Like attending to matters millinery. The history books tell us that much of Florida's exotic bird population was wiped out by hunters in search of feathers for high-fashion hats. And the postcards tell me that my ancestors contributed to the carnage.

"We shall have the annual plume hunt next Sunday," writes my Uncle Ray, in 1909. "Charles has prospected the territory and reports we shall have no problems finding all that you require. We are expecting the same fine luncheon that you have served us in years past. Have you still those strawberry preserves? If not, please make some."

There was even baseball. Back then, each Central Florida town had its own team. Of course, getting from town to town could prove tricky.

"Sorry you could not make it to the baseball game in Eustis," writes my Uncle Stanley in 1906. "We ourselves did not arrive until 5 p.m. as the road was quite muddy. The mules became unhitched and it took three hours to gather them in. We won 31-0, needing only 54 minutes to beat the Eustis boys."

There was exciting news from afar. Well, as afar as Jacksonville anyway.

"We have seen the Duval Theatre and its moving picture machine," writes a correspondent named Mildred. "Now, suppose you can persuade someone in Leesburg to buy one?"

And though I never met my grandfather Morris, I have come to know him through his postcards.

My favorite is one he mailed from Ocala on Oct. 18, 1905. It has to be among the earliest novelty cards, a facetious "Liar's License" certifying that "J.S. Morris is entitled to lie from Oct. 18 to Jan. 1, 1906, being a duly qualified Liar and having passed a thorough examination."

It was received by my grandmother just a week before they were married.

When my parents moved out of their house, I got the postcard albums. My attention never lags whenever I pull them out for a look. I find myself becoming downright fastidious about them, too.

Recently, I met someone who is a serious collector of postcards and told him about the ones I have.

"Sounds as if you might have a number of them that could be worth a good deal of money, if you were ever interested in selling them," he said. "I'd be more than happy to take a look at them."

He has since called twice and written once. Like Mr. E.J. Hamm, maybe he'll soon just take the hint and disappear.

Streak of Gold

....

WE LOAD JEFFREY'S SKIFF IN THE brittle darkness of 5 a.m., then head out Garrison Bight, past the Navy docks, putting the lights of Key West behind us. It's an hour run to the Marquesa Islands. Jeffrey insists that we be fishing by dawn.

"When you see a tarpon breaking at sunrise," he tells my wife and me, "it's like a streak of gold dancing on the water."

The wind is blowing heavy from the south, giving us a wet pounding across Boca Grande Channel. When we reach the Marquesas, Jeffrey tucks into the lee of the westernmost island and cuts the Evinrude. He grabs his 15-foot fiberglass pole, climbs the platform above the motor and pushes us silently across the flats.

The sun is sending out its advance guard, snakey wisps of vermillion and peach. We watch the water, prospecting for streaks of gold ...

Jeffrey Cardenas is an old and good friend from college. We worked together in newspapers for a while, before he gave up journalism and moved to the Keys with his wife. Ginny went to work as an assistant state attorney. And Jeffrey began making a name for himself as a commercial photographer.

But the water always beckoned. The week after he and Ginny were married, Jeffrey loaded up his 21-foot sailboat and headed east out of Fort Lauderdale across the Atlantic to Spain. Solo.

"Ginny needed some peace and quiet to study for the bar exam," he said. "The timing seemed right."

And it seemed right a few years ago when he bought a small used skiff and started fishing the backwaters of the Keys, learning how to sight and stalk bonefish, permit and tarpon. Before long he had his guide's license and was taking out paying customers. He combined the photography with the fishing, shooting artful color pictures of his anglers' catch. It gave them something to take home besides the memories, Jeffrey being a firm believer in releasing every fish.

He got a bigger, better boat. He stopped catching fish on a spinning rod and taught himself to fly fish. Before long he was fly fishing exclusively and had earned a reputation among the sport's die-hard devotees, men and women whose consuming passion is to travel the globe catching game fish with unlikely looking bits of fluff and feather wrapped around a hook, and damn all the costs.

Last year, Jeffrey was named the International Fishing Guide of the Year, only the second guide from Florida ever to win the honor. Between February and July he fishes every day, from before sunup to late afternoon. Some of his anglers have him booked five years in advance.

Still, for Jeffrey, the fishing is utter joy.

As he poles across the flats – stingrays darting off the bow, a nurse shark nosing up food beneath the purple sea fan – Jeffrey tells us stories.

"You should have seen it the first time I came fishing out here with Mango," he says. Mango is his dog, a kindly, sorrowful golden retriever. It was before he started fly fishing and Jeffrey was throwing a Mirrorlure with a treble hook on each end. A big tarpon, maybe 130 to 150 pounds, took the plug near the boat.

"The tarpon roared out of the water, stretched out over us on its tail and Mango leaped out after it," Jeffrey says. "One of the treble hooks was dangling out of the tarpon's mouth and Mango got snagged on that."

The tarpon dove with the dog impaled alongside it. Then dog and fish surfaced, rolled and disappeared.

"I figured that was it, that I'd lost my dog," he says. "A minute or so went by, then I see what looks like a rug floating up from the bottom. Mango came up spitting and wheezing. Not too many dogs have ever jumped with a tarpon. Funny, Mango hasn't seemed real enthusiastic about fishing since then."

A tarpon's most-feared predator is the hammerhead shark, an eating machine that can grow as long as 20 feet. One morning Jeffrey and his angler were closing in on a large school of tarpon when, a couple of hundred yards beyond the fish, they saw a sickle-shaped tail thrash up, followed by a steam-rolling surge of water, like some rogue wave.

"Picture a submarine throwing water off either side, going about

30 miles per hour," Jeffrey says.

He started the engine and sped toward the tarpon, putting his 17-foot boat between them and the hammerhead, noticing the shark was as long as the boat.

In about four feet of water the hammerhead couldn't go under the boat, so whenever it made a move toward the tarpon, Jeffrey would counter it with his boat.

"My angler was screaming, terrified," he says. "He knew for sure that the shark was just going to say to hell with the tarpon and come after us."

It was only a matter of time, though. The hammerhead succeeded in isolating one of the tarpon and, after flipping the fish into the air and pounding it back and forth with each side of its anvil-shaped head, severed its meal in two. While the shark eased away with the lower half, Jeffrey gaffed the head for a photograph.

"The hammerhead saw us and went nuts because we were stealing its food," says Jeffrey, "It was zeroing in, right on us."

They sped off from the flats, a mad hammerhead in pursuit.

And then there was the time one of Jeffrey's anglers fought a 150-pound tarpon for five grueling hours before finally bringing the exhausted fish alongside the boat. When Jeffrey removed the hook and released the tarpon, it spiraled downward.

"We could see it lying belly up in the bottom of a channel, 15 to 20 feet down," Jeffrey said. "It was shark bait."

Jeffrey dove after the tarpon, just knowing a shark was vectoring in. Grabbing the fish he pulled it to shallow water. It took four hours of easing the fish back and forth, forcing water through its gills, until it had the strength to swim away.

There is such a thing as fish karma. Such acts of goodness are repaid. This is the fishing guide's faith.

Suddenly, my wife shouts: "There! There! Tarpon rolling!"

It's a pod of five or six males, circling a big, spawning female. They are truly golden in the morning light. And all I can do is stand there gawking at them.

"It's your shot, pal," says Jeffrey.

I work out my line with the red, feathery fly that Jeffrey tied special the night before. My cast lands right in the middle of the tarpon.

There's a flash through the water. And ... well, that's another story.

Another Fish Story

THOSE LUCKY FOLKS WHO HAVE survived tornadoes report that their first clue came from the awful sound. Like a freight train, they said.

What I heard sounded more like a Hoover upright vacuum cleaner. But it was still plenty terrifying. Especially when I looked out on the not-so-distant cloud bank and saw the spiraling gray funnel that had speared the Gulf of Mexico, a wicked umbilical seeking earthly attachment.

A waterspout.

It was maybe a mile away, sucking up whatever it pleased. If I'd been on land I could have hunkered down. If I'd been in a boat I could have high-tailed it elsewhere.

But no. I was dead in the water, on my sailboard, fishing rod in hand. I was easy pickings, too far from the Boca Grande shore to do anything but watch . . . and try to project my landfall when it came time for the waterspout to spit me out.

All because I was trying to perfect a brand-new sport. All because I was anxious to become the Father of Windfishing.

The hell of it was: In the lull before the big blow, the wind had died and I was stranded in the middle of the bay, on the backside of a skinny barrier island. The fish weren't biting and, even if they were, I was too distracted to go after them. Funny how impending death tends to galvanize your attention.

The waterspout sliced in from the Gulf, its tail retracting as it approached the shore. And I thought, maybe, just maybe, I was safe.

But no sooner had the churning squall line crossed over the island to the bay than the dervish came whirling down again.

You know how it is when you go to the fair and order cotton candy and the vendor sticks the cardboard tube into the machine and twirls it while the wispy fluff keeps growing bigger and bigger and bigger?

That's sort of what it's like staring into a descending waterspout.

I've read that many good people of ancient Pompeii turned in their escape from raging Vesuvius and, frozen by the horrendous beauty, became lawn ornaments for the ages.

Likewise, I froze . . .

I got the idea for my brand-new sport this past summer while windsurfing over some flats near the mouth of Tampa Bay, where the water is still clear and the turtle grass thick. There were fish everywhere. And I was powerless to catch them. You'd have to be a fisherman to understand just how frustrating this can be.

There have been other times when on a fruitless fishing trip (most of mine are like that) the wind has blown up nicely and I've been powerless to do anything about that either. You'd have to be a windsurferperson to understand just how frustrating this can be.

Surely, there had to be a way . . .

All it took was a bungee cord. I strapped my spinning outfit onto the stern of my sailboard and headed back to the flats.

There were two boats drifting through the area where I'd spotted all the fish. I pulled up between them, dropped sail and, sitting on the board with my feet dangling in the water, began casting.

The fishermen on the boats eyed me with even more suspicion than fishermen normally accord each other. I'm reasonably sure the term "damn fool" came up in their conversation.

Finally, one of them hollered: "Been some good size sharks in here."

I was cool, way cool.

"Sharks are supposed to be here," I hollered back.

"That may be," said the fisherman, "but whatchu gonna do when you hook up with one of them?"

I am the Father of Windfishing. And I am not too proud to admit that there are some kinks in the sport that still need smoothing out.

Surprise, surprise. I escaped death by waterspout. It touched down a quarter-mile beyond me, siphoning up who-knows-what from the bay. Later that afternoon, some unsuspecting soul was probably standing in his back yard 20 miles inland, only to be suddenly showered with mullet and jellyfish and mad blue crabs. Nature does enjoy its practical jokes.

All I know is that fishing is good in the wake of a waterspout. And windfishing is even better. The breeze that followed the turmoil was easy on my mediocre windsurfing skills, the fish so bite-happy that even I could catch them. As a fisherman or a windsurfer, separate and apart, I'd rank low on accomplishment. But as a windfisherman I am second to none. At least, while this sport of mine is in its infancy.

I was casting a silver spoon and in less than an hour I caught, I swear, four trout, two redfish, two ladyfish, a needlefish, one grunt and four feisty mangrove snapper. I threw them all back.

That's one of the major flaws with windfishing. No storage space. I'd hang a stringer with my catch off the side of the board but, well, I do have this little hang-up about shark bait.

But . . . why not rig a little ice chest near the mast? That way, there'd be beer at hand, too. And maybe a couple of rod holders, one fore and one aft. And a live well. And one of those electronic fish-finders. And some outriggers and a flying bridge?

Surely, there has to be a way . . .

Sydney van Dyke

SYDNEY VAN DYKE, 13, OF Maitland died Friday after a long illness.

A professional cat of the Burmese variety, Sydney was well-known in his heyday as a relentless stalker of birds and was a chief contributor to the decline of the ground dove population in Maitland. His field of interest also extended to blue jays, mockingbirds and an occasional squirrel.

Sydney was a member in good standing of the Florida Chapter of Lizards Unlimited, a group of sporting felines dedicated to wreaking perpetual havoc and torture upon blue-tailed skinks, green anoles, chameleons and whatever exotic Reptilia dare scamper in back yards.

Ever the innovator, Sydney is credited with inventing "Lizard Hockey." After capturing a lizard, Sydney would then race from one end of the back porch to the other, slapping the lizard from paw to paw across the smooth tile floor, often attempting a difficult ricochet shot off a terra-cotta pot to thrill whatever spectators might be watching.

The lizards, thoroughly stunned by the experience, would then be subjected to one of Sydney's ongoing biological experiments.

A noted expert in lizard physiology, Sydney would first remove a portion of a lizard's tail, then study how the lizard got along without it. After a few minutes, he would recapture the lizard and remove a leg. The experiment proceeded until the lizard was, basically, a quintuple amputee, at which point Sydney would graciously donate his research findings to the public, usually by depositing the lizard's carcass in someone's shoe.

Born in North Fort Myers, Fla., (sire: Danela Krishnateps, dam: Morry's Astor Belle) Sydney took up residency in the Morris household a couple of years before the secondary occupants began having children. He was named after Sydney (last name unknown), owner of Sydney's Peace & Love Restaurant on the island of Jost van Dyke in the British Virgins.

Sydney (the restaurant owner) had 12 sons whom he named Sydney 2, Sydney 3, Sydney 4, etc. The Morrises figured the original Sydney probably would not mind having a Burmese cat thrown into the lineage.

The appellation was fitting since Sydney (the cat) developed what can only be described as a Caribbean attitude. Never hurried, always willing to put off until tomorrow what could be done today, Sydney devoted the bulk of his time to finding which window in the house let in the most sunlight. Then he would bask in it.

He was a perpetual purrer. And, when petted, the sound increased to just short of a chain saw. He liked a good stomach rub and a scratch under the chin. But massage his backbone, just forward of his tail, and he was yours forever.

Sydney achieved some degree of fame as a performer, going by the stage name of "Sydney, the Sausage Cat." To entertain guests, Mr. Morris would often lift up Sydney, stretch the cat out and say something like: "Doesn't he look like one of those 10-pound salamis you see hanging in a deli?"

Mr. Morris would then drape Sydney over his head where he would hang limp and do his impersonation of a pair of earmuffs.

"I have never seen another cat who would put up with such a humiliating thing," observers often remarked.

This tolerance extended toward children. The Morris children often mistook Sydney for a stuffed animal, dragging him all over the house by his tail. Still, he would curl up in their beds at night. And he was subjected to countless "Show and Tell" sessions in elementary school classrooms, never once hissing or clawing.

Two years ago he was diagnosed as suffering from the feline version of Acquired Immune Deficiency Syndrome, probably the result of a nasty scrap with a mean black cat that hasn't been seen since. In the last month Sydney had failed considerably, losing weight, eyesight and continence. A trip to the vet ended his misery.

A burial ceremony was conducted in the back yard of the Morris home, with eulogies offered by all.

"Bye-bye, my buddy," said the older Morris boy.

"You were the greatest cat ever," said the younger.

Sydney's grave is under a palm tree. It has a fine, unobstructed view of the bird feeder. When I looked out there the other morning, all the lizards were giving it wide berth.

My New Highway Policy

• •

I WOULD LIKE TO TAKE THIS OPPORTUNITY TO ANNOUNCE MY new highway policy.

This is, of course, in response to recent grumblings from my associates that I do not have a highway policy.

"Why are you driving so slow?" asks the 8-year-old.

"We'll never get there the rate you're going," observes the 9-year-old.

They suspect I am trying to torture them. They think I have become, if not an old fogey, then at least a middle-aged one. They have the backing of their mother.

"I swear this is the absolute last trip I am taking anywhere where you are driving," she announced during the last trip she took with me anywhere I drove. "Would you please hurry up?"

It was Thanksgiving. We were driving 180 miles to eat turkey with her family.

Now I realize that many otherwise sane people, when faced with a journey of 180 miles, will allot themselves a precise time in which to make it.

"We can average 60 miles per hour and make it in three hours," they'll reckon. "If we miss rush hour through Tampa and if the highway patrol isn't out on I-75."

But they don't take into consideration certain variables. Like, why should anyone be in such a big hurry to eat turkey? We'll leave the fact that it's with "her family" out of it.

Besides, if I am going anywhere even remotely near Tampa, then I usually like to make a brief side trip to Ybor City and the Silver Ring Cafe for the Cuban Especial Sandwich and a crab roll with hot sauce. And if I have detoured all the way to Ybor City then it just naturally makes sense to head on to St. Petersburg and cross Tampa Bay on the Sunshine Skyway, one of the most thrilling spectacles in all of Florida, especially if it's time for sunset. If it's not time for sunset then I generally dawdle over a plate of mackerel or mullet at Ted Peters' Smokehouse until it is.

Okay, so the 180-mile trip winds up taking six hours. At least once you arrive you aren't so hungry that you'll even eat turkey. Plus, you don't run the risk of facing "her family" on an empty stomach.

This is my new highway policy: We'll get there. Sooner or later.

Actually, that was my old highway policy, too. Traveling, it seems to me, is best accomplished through a series of side trips. But under my old highway policy I would do my traveling, even the side trips, at a high rate of speed. Under my new highway policy I drive slow.

"Daddy," observed one of my associates on our last trip, "you are driving like an old person."

Exactly. Driving like an old person is at the very core of my new highway policy. My new highway policy was inspired by old people.

As you might have noticed there are a lot of old people in Florida. I have been studying their driving habits for years. Perhaps "studying" isn't the word we're looking for here. Perhaps "cussing" is. At any rate, after years of cussing the driving habits of the old people in Florida, it recently occurred to me, while traveling at a high rate of speed down the highway, weaving around old people in their cars as if they were stanchions on a slalom course, that old people might be on to something.

"How did all those old people get to be old people?" I asked myself.

It was one of those cosmic revelations that, for some reason, made a hell of a lot more sense at the moment it was revealed to me than when I just put it down in cold, hard print. But the gist of it was: Slow down.

Another thing: Study the faces of people who try to get someplace in a hurry on the highway. Note the grim countenance, the furrowed brow. These are people who grind their teeth in bed at night, swig more than their share of antacids and probably beat their dogs. Their entire range of facial expression is from scowl to sneer to snarl. Not a pretty sight.

Study the faces of old people going slow on the highway. Some of them actually smile. Their placidity is Buddha-like. Granted, this placidity can also be interpreted as – Totally Oblivious to What's Going on Around Them. But more and more, as far as Florida highways are concerned, being totally oblivious to what's going on around you seems a reasonable option. Besides, I fully intend to be an old person some day. Why not start training now?

This is not to say I have adopted all the driving habits of old people in Florida. My new highway policy does not include:

• Making abrupt left-hand turns any time I damn well feel like it.

• Driving a large Buick.

• Making all the old women ride in the back seat of my large Buick while us old guys ride up front.

But I am driving slow and I like it. Driving slow is helping me do something I haven't been able to do in a very long time. Since 99 percent of all the cars on the highway pass me, I am now at leisure to identify them by make and model. I haven't been able to do this since, oh, about 1967 when life was simpler and cars had real names like Impala or Cougar or Comet. The other day I successfully identified an Acura. Before, I had mistaken Acuras for Ultimas, Maximas and Luminas. Although I'm still not clear on Luminas. I might be mistaking them for a new brand of cigarettes. But I hope to achieve a new sense of order by driving slow and identifying cars.

My associates are helping me.

"Oh no! We are getting passed by a Geezer Pleaser," the 8-year-old shouted on a recent outing. "This is awful. A Geezer Pleaser is going faster than we are."

A Geezer Pleaser? I wasn't familiar with that model. And, to tell you the truth, the car that passed us looked suspiciously like a large Buick. I nodded at the occupants whose combined ages surpassed several centuries.

Handsome car, that Geezer Pleaser. Might just have to give one a test drive. It has a large back seat. Plenty of room for my associates.

Just Keeping Score

WE ARE SITTING IN THE stadium at Baseball City, watching the Royals and the Reds from some good seats behind home plate, when along about the third inning the guy in front of me turns around and asks: "Say, what did Brett do his last time up?"

I glance back two innings in my scorebook.

"Hit the 0-1 pitch into a double play," I say. "A 6-4-3."

The guy in front of me eyes the worn, white-jacketed ring binder in my lap and the No. 2 pencil that begins each game unblemished but winds up gnawed and flaking yellow paint.

"You're a pretty serious scorekeeper, huh?"

"Nothing that serious about it," I say. "But, yeah, I keep score."

Just then, George Brett taps a puny, little dribbler toward the Reds' first baseman, who picks it up, touches the bag and the inning is over.

It is duly noted in my score book: "3-Upld."

My younger son, the 8-year-old, is an apprentice scorekeeper.

"I know that '3-U' means the first baseman made the play unassisted," he says. "But what's that 'pld' mean?"

"Stands for puny, little dribbler," I tell him.

It's my score book. I can keep score however I want. All that really matters is: I keep score.

Halfway through my last year on the Leesburg High School baseball team, Coach Buddy Lowe handed me the team score book and suggested that I could best serve the Fightin' Yellow Jackets by keeping score. I was not offended. I was a marginal player at best – weak glove, weaker bat, pretty decent speed if only I could get on base. I was best at chatter: "Heybatter-nobatter-heybatter-nobatter-hey-swing!!!!"

There were some good young players coming up. It was time I stepped out and made room for them. Such is the cycle of baseball. My playing career ended at 18. And I began learning the intricacies of keeping a score book.

It was a skill that paid off. Indeed, the ability to keep a baseball score book helped determine what passes for my destiny.

Back then Leesburg had a team in the Class A Florida State League. Coach Lowe was the official scorer. And when he couldn't make it to a game he called on me to substitute.

The official scorer was in charge of the press box, not nearly as prestigious as it might sound since the official scorer was usually the only person in the press box. But it meant I was also in charge of the PA system. I got to play a scratched copy of the National Anthem over the loudspeaker, run the scoreboard and announce the batters as they stepped to the plate.

After the game I phoned in results to the newspapers and wire services. I had to think up a one-sentence summary of the game, something like: "Cletus Bohunkus slapped a three-run homer and a double to lead the Leesburg Athletics to a 7-4 win over the Daytona Beach Dodgers Friday night." For this I got $5 from *The Orlando Sentinel*, $5 from the *Tampa Tribune* and $10 from The Associated Press. Add to that the $10 the team paid me and I was making $30 ... just for watching a game of baseball.

Not too many years afterward I found myself in serious need of a profession. Playing first base for the Yankees was no longer an option. Is it any wonder I chose the newspaper business – a line of work that routinely paid people big money for doing, essentially, nothing?

OK, so maybe the years have proved me wrong about the money part. But it's what I do. I owe it all to baseball. And, whenever I go to a game, I still keep score.

The mechanics of scorekeeping are so simple that most anyone with a bare knowledge of baseball can learn to keep a score book through the course of a single game. Each player is assigned a number according to position (pitcher is 1, catcher is 2, first baseman is 3, and so on). Then all you do is follow the ball. The batter flies out to the right fielder? Score it an "F-9." Strikes out swinging? It's a "K." Strikes out looking? A backward "K."

Say the runner on first base heads toward second then gets caught in a rundown with the catcher throwing it to the second baseman who throws it to the first baseman who throws it to the shortstop who is backing up the second baseman who throws it to the catcher who is backing up the first baseman who throws it to the second baseman for the out? Score it a 2-4-3-6-2-4.

In no other sport can a game be reduced to such an explicit shorthand. You can sit down with a well-kept baseball score book and follow the action pitch-by-pitch. There is order and explanation and an irrefutable sense of logic – commodities sorely lacking in the world at large. Just one more reason why I like to keep score.

Bottom of the ninth. The score is tied, 2-2, with the Royals at bat. This will be the final game for the score book I have kept over the last couple of years. Its pages are filled. I'll get a new score book this month to start the new season.

I have spent a goodly part of the afternoon reviewing old games. The scorebook is more than just a sports record. It is a journal. And its margins are filled with scribbled memories . . .

From a Dodgers-Met game in Vero Beach: "The boys are pouting because Tommy Lasorda wouldn't give them his autograph."

From a Red Sox-Twins game last spring, the final Twins game at Tinker Field: "Lucky day! Bo and Dash got picked from the crowd to be bat boys."

From an Orlando SunRays game last summer: "Old fellow in front of me just told me he was from Alaquippa, Pa., home of Henry Mancini, Tony Dorsett and Mike Ditka. Says I ought to visit sometime."

And from this very game: "The day after Bo Jackson left the Royals. I ran into my old high school principal, Buford Robinson. And I realize that, at 40, I am about the same age as Mr. Robinson when he was my principal. Back then I thought he was ancient. Am horrified."

Then there's the rifle shot of a line drive to left. Kevin Seitzer has knocked in the winning run. I score it, close the book and we head home.

The Inscrutable Porch Creature

I ONCE HAD A neighbor I called Porch Creature. I did not know his real name. He lived five houses down from me.

There was a sign in his front yard – like something you'd have custom-made at a flea market – that said, "The Old Homestead." It showed a happy couple holding hands and waving at passersby.

And yet, I could not muster even a nod from Porch Creature, much less a wave or a hello. I would walk by his house, give him a "Hey, howya doin'?" and he would just sit there, staring out from a rocker on his screened porch, a large, dour, crewcut man in his 60s, given to plaid flannel shirts and overalls.

He was neither catatonic nor immobile. Occasionally, I would see him working in his yard, yelling something inside to his wife. Sometimes she would join him on the porch. I would hear the two of them talking as I approached on my walk. They would spot me and there would be silence.

We lived in a small Florida town. One stoplight, fewer than 1,000 people, 20 miles to the nearest movie or fast food joint.

We had fled the congestion of South Florida, looking for a place where there was, essentially, nothing. The town exceeded all expectations. There was nothing and then some. It was the kind of town where newcomers were not immediately embraced. Folks were friendly enough, but they required some time to size you up. I had no problem with this. I am much the same way about strangers. The friends we eventually made there were good ones.

But Porch Creature was something else again. After a year or so of unrequited greetings, I resorted to facetiousness.

"How the heck ya doin'?" I would say, with far too much enthusiasm.

By the time the third year came around, we had made plans to move from the small town and Porch Creature could sit and rot in his rocker for all I cared. I still spoke to him whenever I walked by. But I had become surly about it.

"Hey, howya doin'?" I'd say. Then, in an aside quite loud enough for him to hear: "Great, I'm just fine, too. Thanks for asking. Yep, it is a nice day."

Not even an arched eyebrow from Porch Creature. He just sat and stared.

On this Easter Sunday past, we had planned a trip to the beach. But it rained. It had rained on Friday and Saturday, too. Perhaps people who live in Seattle have evolved to a point where they can deal civilly with unending days of gray and wetness.

Floridians haven't.

We prefer our rain in two-hour doses, thank you very much. Flash, bang, squall and torrent. Get the downpour over with and let us hurry up and have some sun. Else we tend to turn slightly manic.

Which is to say, my wife and kids and I were at each other's throats come Easter Sunday afternoon. Petty sniping was the order of the day, until my wife displayed that innate sense of womanly reasonableness that caused me to marry her in the first place.

"Let's all go for a walk in the rain," she said.

It was, of course, the perfect thing to do. The kids, who had objected mightily at first, soon discovered that Mom and Dad weren't going to rein them in at mud puddles. They waded. They stomped. They splashed. We joined them.

We wore raincoats, but still we got wet. I found myself wondering how the expression, "You're all wet," came to be a put-down and vowed to use it only with admiration in the future. Baptismal analogies aside, the decision to go out and get wet when all others sit safe and dry seems, at the very least, plucky and, by the furthest stretch, noble.

It's just that you come off goofy. People passing in their cars gave us the weirdest looks, drop-jawed and bug-eyed. Yet there was that occasional glimmer of connection, the glance that said: "Why yes, walking in the rain on a day like today does make absolute sense. By God, that's what I should be doing."

We wound up walking twice as far as we had planned. And when we arrived back home, I won't go so far as to say we were transformed by the experience. But at least we got along. That's all you can ask. That's what a walk in the rain can do for you.

On the Sunday before we moved out of the small town, my wife and I left the kids at home with a sitter and went on a long, goodbye walk. We were gone a couple of hours. The clouds built up in a hurry. It rained and rained hard. We were soaked by the time we made it back to our street. I could see Porch Creature sitting in his rocker. And I decided then and there, to hell with it, I am going to snub him just like he has been snubbing me. No more Mr. Friendly Bob. I am leaving this town and putting that ungracious lump behind me.

We reached the sidewalk in front of Porch Creature's house. I did not even glance his way. So long, sucker. Have a nice life. Then, out of the corner of my eye, I saw Porch Creature get up from his rocker, walk to the edge of the porch and peer out the screen.

He hollered: "Kinda wet out ain't it?"

We stopped. I looked at him. He was grinning, observing us like we were perfect fools.

He hollered again: "Ain't got enough sense to come in out of the rain?"

He cracked himself up. He tossed his head back, rocked on his heels and laughed. He was the only person I've ever heard who, when he laughed, actually went: "Hee-hee-hee."

I said: "No, don't suppose we got much sense at all."

And that cracked up Porch Creature even more. I knew what he was going to say next and he said it.

"Good day for ducks, isn't it? Hee-hee-hee ... "

He stood there shaking his head and grinning at us. We grinned back, then started walking toward our house.

"Be seeing you," said Porch Creature. He waved. He actually waved.

"Be seeing you," I said and waved back.

"Nice old fellow," said my wife.

"Yeah," I said. "I'll miss him."

We left town the next day. And I think about the sorry old fool every time I go walking in the rain.

Exotic
Floridians

●●●●●●●●●●●●●●●●●●●●●●●●●●●

IT WAS 200 YEARS AGO that British naturalist William Bartram published a historic account of his travels through Florida.

"This remarkable land doth provide a divine wealth of species," he wrote in *The Travels of William Bartram*. "It is a diverse earthly paradise defying all mortal imagination."

Inspired by Bartram's entrancement, John James Audubon ventured down to our peninsula in the winter of 1831-32, painting as he went. Ever the stickler for authenticity, Audubon was not content to make his famed sketches of flamingos and roseate spoonbills from afar. When he wanted to classify and paint a bird, he went out and shot it. All the better for studying wing, beak and feather up close.

The present-day society that bears his name would probably revoke John James Audubon's membership for decimating the bird population the way he did. But back then, with Florida so vast and mysterious, such behavior was acceptable. Killing all those birds was a way to help understand what was here. The times called for it. Besides, the Audubon Society Field Guide to North American Birds has become highly profitable.

Some two centuries later, Florida remains vast and mysterious. But bird and beast are outnumbered by creatures of a more aggravating, insidious nature. And clearly, the times call for someone to step forward and help others understand the divine wealth of species this remarkable land doth nowadays provide.

That's why I am delighted to share with you a few entries from my latest work-in-progress – The Morris Society Field Guide to Floridians. I offer it as proof that, while this place we call home may fall short of earthly paradise, its inhabitants still defy all mortal imagination. A few most unnatural selections from phylum Floridae:

Retirus outtasortus (Common name: Condo-dwelling, liver-spotted grouch) – An easily spooked creature who seems to thrive upon being at odds with his neighbors. Might once have been tolerable, even likable, but has evolved to a high level of disagreeability by living in close quarters with others who have too much time on their hands.

Most common activities: going to meetings of the condo association by-laws committee, complaining about the monthly maintenance fee, and scoping out restaurants that offer "Early Bird" discounts.

Identifying call: "So waddaya mean your grandkids are going to come stay with you for two weeks? The association rules clearly state that there is a one-week limit."

Flora margarita (Common name: Flower-shirted tequila guzzler) – A deeply tanned individual, exclusively male, who has bought the Jimmy Buffett fantasy lock, stock and hangover. Friendly and outgoing, especially when you are buying.

Greatest anxiety: deciding whether to call his pet parrot "Reefer" or "Cheeseburger."

Most common activities: pretending to know something about sailing, demanding the house band play "Margaritaville" and wondering why Buffett never wrote a song that warned about skin cancer.

Identifying call: "So darling, why don't we get drunk and ... "

Gimmemy commissioni (Common name: Real estate agent) – An extremely prolific species that now accounts for roughly every third person in Florida. Can easily be attracted simply by placing a "For Sale by Owner" sign in your front yard.

Most common activities: memorizing amortization tables, trying to figure out what's going on at closings, and explaining to prospective buyers why the house with a view of the retention pond can justifiably be described as "waterfront."

Identifying call: "I guarantee you'll be able to turn right around and sell this place for $20,000 more than you paid for it."

Pixsixus lowrentus (Common name: Lotto trash) – Former white trash who have cashed in on the Florida Lottery.

Most common activities: learning how to pronounce "annuity," finally paying off all the stuff on Wal-Mart layaway and trying to decide who should get the old double-wide.

Identifying call: "Darla Jo, if I told you once I told you a million times, keep them pigs outta the hot tub."

Igot mines (Common name: Beach hogs) – Well-to-do types who, having secured large oceanfront homes, would deny beach access to everyone else.

Most common activities: answering phones at the Coastal Erosion Telethon and placing land mines in strategic sand crab holes.

Identifying call: "You realize, of course, that I pay taxes on everything past the mean high tide line."

Marsupio touristo (Common name: Pouch people) – A most recent subspecies of the common tourist, marked by insistence upon wearing those silly-looking Gortex mini-packs that fasten around the waist and make the wearers resemble kangaroos on holiday. Where once these ubiquitous belly bags were confined to photographers and schoolchildren, the trait has become so widespread that entire Pouch people families are now regularly sighted. However, most are cheerful and, if asked, will hop on command.

Identifying call: "Say, Myrtle, is the room key in your pouch or mine?"

Sand Castles for the Soul

WE WENT TO THE BEACH THE other day and like always I built a sand castle.

I usually go to the beach with my kids. This gives the appearance that the sand castle is for them. And they do enjoy it.

But the sand castle is really for me. I get a lot out of building sand castles. It is cheap. It is fun. And it cleanses the soul. Whatever nagging baggage I take with me to the beach – worries, fears, anxieties, those bitter nuts we all chew daily – seems lighter when I leave. Sand castles just make me feel good.

In fact, I've even considered starting one of those self-improvement courses that always are popping up. I would call it "sand castle therapy." People would pay me lots of money and I would take them to the beach and show them how building sand castles will straighten out all their psychological entanglements and emotional distress.

It certainly makes as much sense as walking barefooted across beds of hot coals or whatever other foolishness the self-awareness types are up to. People who walk barefooted across hot coals say it teaches them that the determined individual can accomplish anything. What it teaches me is that some people are accomplished fools and there always will be determined individuals who can trick them into doing anything.

There's nothing tricky about building sand castles. The most important task: picking a good spot. Build it too close to the water and it will get washed away before you can fully enjoy it. Build it too far from the water and there is no risk involved, no excitement.

In this respect – and here comes something profound – building a sand castle is like leading a good life. Both require measures of risk before you can fully enjoy them, before they have any worth.

After you pick a good spot, what you must do next is dig a hole and get yourself into it. Again, this is something that anyone who has tried to lead a good life can appreciate. Indeed, I happen to think that the best time to build a sand castle is when one has gotten one's self into a hole and is not quite sure how to get out of it. Building a sand castle offers constructive escape.

It is with a vengeance that I dig holes for my sand castles because I like the sensation of striking water. I don't know exactly what it is about this that I find so thrilling. Maybe it's knowing that I have made contact with a different level of this Earth, that I have broken through the shell and plunged my hands into the core. Anyway, once the hole caves in and gets big enough I sit there with my feet in the water, scooping up sand and building the wall.

Building the wall ... I guess this strikes at the essence of sand castle therapy. You build your wall and thereby create a separate world that you must protect from the rage of the sea.

Of course, the sea isn't really the sea. When I was a kid, the sea was wave after wave of marauding barbarians and I was a Roman emperor defending my empire. I would sit there, surrounded by my wall, hunkered down in my hole, pitted head-to-head against the enemy.

I no longer consider myself an emperor. But there still are barbarians that must be dealt with. We're all confronted by them. And so the sea becomes any and all things with which we must do battle – people at work, neighbors, rivals, the government or just some big, ugly undefinable thing that is lurking somewhere in the back of our minds.

Some people get frilly with their sand castles. Not me. My castles are strictly utilitarian, more fortresses than castles, really. While other castle builders spend time dribbling goop into an elaborate filigree of towers and spires and minarets and such, I build cannonballs. Sounds horribly violent, feels terribly good. I take pride in my arsenal. I mold a dozen or so cannonballs (wet sand on the inside, powdered with dry sand for sting), line the inside of my walls with them and when the waves attack I fire. Ka-blowie, ka-boom! Take that! And that! If my walls are still standing I make more ammunition and fire again. On and on it goes.

Sooner or later, of course, the sea always wins. You must accept this before building any sand castle. Eventually your walls must crumble.

But the good thing about sand castles is that you can just get up and walk away from them. You can shake off the sand and wash your hands clean. You can prepare for the battles that rage elsewhere.

Local Hero

• • • • • • • • • • • • • • • •

WE WERE VISITING OUT-OF-TOWN friends when my youngest son bounced off a trampoline and broke his arm. He walked into the house, cradling this suddenly foreign limb as if it were a hurt puppy.

"It is not broken," he insisted with the patented obstinacy of an 8-year-old. But there was little doubt about it. Between elbow and wrist, his left arm took a sickening dip and an abrupt turn. Gave me the shudders just to look at it.

We were 100 miles from home. The arm couldn't wait until we could return to the family doctor. So we applied ice in a hurry, and Dash and I headed for the nearest hospital.

"It's going to be all right," I told him.

We sat in a curtained cubicle of the emergency room. On one side, a man with his foot wrapped in bloody bandages was telling a nurse about his encounter with a chain saw. On the other side, a teen-age boy held a washcloth against one eye, victim of a tree limb. Across the room, a woman on a stretcher thrashed about and wailed: "It hurts! Ohhhhh, help me!" They wheeled her away.

Dash took it all in. "No, it's not going to be all right," he sobbed. "It's not going to be all right at all."

I hugged him and tried to make it better. I told him about the time when I was 10 and fell out of Jeff Cherry's treehouse, breaking my left arm. I told him that hundreds of little boys break their arms every day and that young bones heal in a hurry. Nothing worked.

"I'm scared, Daddy," he moaned. "I'm real scared."

I hugged him some more. There is no deeper sense of helplessness than that of parents unable to ease their child's pain.

The doctor arrived. Gray-haired, in his 50s. Smiling, soft-spoken.

A doctor from central casting. The orthopedist on call, he had left a backyard family barbecue.

"Sunday afternoons certainly are exciting, aren't they?" he commiserated with me. Then to Dash: "So tell me how it happened, young man."

And as the doctor took Dash's arm into his hand, I felt the tension leave my son's body. Dash took a deep breath, relaxed and reported the details while the doctor gently probed the break. The doctor explained his findings to my son, not me.

"You've broken both bones, young man," he said. "But it's going to be all right."

The exact same thing I'd told Dash. Only this time he accepted it.

Waiting for the nurse to bring in all the bone-setting paraphernalia, the doctor and I sat and talked.

"So what do you do?" he asked.

"I write a newspaper column," I told him.

"You know," he said, "I've always wanted to be a writer."

I hear that a lot. Mostly from people who consider writing a quaint hobby, like knitting or needlepoint. But before I could hit him with my stock, fit-the-occasion reply ("Really? Gee, I've always wanted to be an orthopedic surgeon.") he was pursuing the thought.

"You know what I'd write about if I had a newspaper column?" he asked. "I'd write about heroes. You got any heroes?"

"No one comes to mind in a hurry," I said.

"That's the problem. People who become famous these days aren't real heroes. And the real heroes – no one ever hears about. I'd search out the heroes – people who make a big difference doing small things in their everyday lives. And I'd write about them.

"Our kids," and he nodded toward Dash, "need to grow up having real heroes."

We talked about the importance of everyday heroes and how our respective professions weren't widely viewed as breeding grounds for the heroic.

"Doctors are made out to be money-grubbing incompetents," he said.

"And all journalists," I said, "are cynics and charlatans."

The nurse arrived with a big needle and the makings for the cast.

"It's going to sting, but you can take it, Dash," said the doctor. When the broken arm was numb, he set the bones and wrapped the cast while he and Dash talked about football. The arm is going to be all right.

"Try to write about some heroes from time to time," said the doctor.

I assured him I would. His name is Dr. Steve Gilman. He lives in Ocala. He would never nominate himself for herohood, I'm sure. But, please, allow me . . .

Jellyfish du jour

IN THE EVENT MY LOVING family decides to file charges against me, I'd just like to mention, for the record, that I meant no harm in making them eat a jellyfish.

Actually, I am not altogether clear on whether it was a single jellyfish they ate or a bunch of them. The package it came in just said: "Dried Salted Jellyfish." And since the jellyfish(es) had been conveniently shredded into long strands – it looked like a package of sauerkraut – it was difficult to determine the exact number of jellyfish involved. Besides, you know how it is with jellyfish. They are not the sort of lower life form to stand up and be counted. They are spineless.

All I know is that I had it on good authority that not only was "Dried Salted Jellyfish" edible, it was something of a delicacy.

"Oh yes, jellyfish very, very good," Cuong Quach told me. "My children ask me all the time can we please soon eat more jellyfish?"

Cuong Quach owns the Vietnamese grocery store where I sometimes shop. It is a Vietnamese grocery store by virtue of the fact that Cuong Quach is originally from Saigon (he owned a grocery store there, too), although the food on his shelves comes from all parts Oriental.

Like the Pickled Mud Fish (Thailand). Or the Bird's Nest Drink (Singapore). Or the Longevity Noodles (China).

That's the thing about shopping at Cuong Quach's grocery store. Spot an item like Longevity Noodles and I have to buy it. Plain old macaroni pales beside such an offering.

At Cuong Quach's grocery store I buy food just because it is curious, just because I have to know how anyone anywhere could eat such stuff, just because it is there. This explains why I have come home with such tasty treats as White Fungus with Lotus Nut (Philippines) and Chicken Essence Candy (China) and, one of my favorites, the extremely versatile Cuttlefish Jerky Dried In Its Own Ink (Taiwan), which comes with the entreaty: "Much enjoy for snack, picnic or party time!" Don't laugh. The Taiwanese probably snicker at the concept of Cheez Doodles.

I think I had shown remarkable restraint in not breaking down and buying the Dried Salted Jellyfish before I did. You must admit, it is a remarkable concept. I always figured that if you dried a jellyfish you wound up with, basically, nothing. Like dehydrated water.

But . . . there are lots of jellyfish in Florida waters. So if it turned out that my loving family went wild over jellyfish, then we'd always find an abundant supply. And we could have jellyfish harvesting excursions, a real family bonding experience. Plus, jellyfish are the main food of sea turtles, which often live to be hundreds of years old. Jellyfish are probably very good for you.

Anyway, that was my line of reasoning when I bought the Dried Salted Jellyfish. I expect my attorney might bring it out in my defense at the trial.

How to prepare jellyfish (in the words of Cuong Quach): "Good thing about jellyfish is that you no need cook it. All you do is take it from package and wash it several times in cold water. Very important: Make sure it is cold water. Do not use hot water. Hot water very bad for jellyfish. Then sprinkle some sesame oil on jellyfish and put it in refrigerator. Then you cook maybe some pork or some chicken or some shrimp and some vegetables like carrots maybe. And then you mix together some soy sauce and some oyster sauce and a little sugar and put that on the meat and vegetables. Then you put the meat and vegetables on top of the jellyfish. But again, very important: Do not heat jellyfish. If jellyfish gets hot it taste like rubber bands."

I had every intention of sitting down for dinner with my loving family so that we could all eat the jellyfish together. Really. But you know how it is in these hectic modern times in which we live.

I made the jellyfish just like Cuong Quach said (I went with the pork) and it was all sitting in the refrigerator when suddenly I remembered that I was supposed to be somewhere at 7 p.m. and it was already 6:30 and my wife wasn't home from work yet and I'd never make it unless I got moving and . . .

So while I hurried to change clothes I called the boys to the table and served them big heaping plates of pork and carrots and jellyfish. No, I did not tell them what it was. Again, my line of reasoning: If I told them it was jellyfish and they refused to eat it, then I was in a hurry to leave and didn't have anything else to feed them and they'd go hungry. Honest, your honor. I thought I was being a responsible parent. Besides, the boys liked it. They asked for seconds.

Before I left, I wrote a note to my wife telling her that dinner was in the refrigerator. In big letters I wrote: "DO NOT HEAT. EAT COLD." I didn't mention anything about how if she ignored that it would taste like rubber bands.

I got home late that night. Everyone was asleep. I was hungry. I checked the refrigerator. All the jellyfish was gone. Every bit of it.

Now, I had planned to eat some of it myself. Honest. My motive was absolutely pure. I swear. I would never, ever trick my loving family into eating jellyfish.

"Sick!" was all my older son, Bo, could say when I came clean the next day. "I am going to sue you!"

"I am calling HRS," said Dash, the younger one. "That is child abuse."

My wife still hasn't spoken. Nothing, not even an offer of a tasty Bird's Nest Drink, seems to appease her.

The History of Weather

IN THE BEGINNING THERE was weather. And it was good. The high was always 78 with a low of 62, and it rained only when necessary but never on weekends or legal holidays or during important baseball games or when your clothes were on the line.

No one talked about the weather then because it was always the same. And this was good, too. A lot of people who might have said things like "Hot enough for you?" or "Good day for ducks, isn't it?" found conversation tough and were reduced to nodding their heads and smiling a lot.

And then something caused a ripple in the gene pool of humanity, and out slithered someone who took one look at the sky and said: "Tomorrow's high will be 78, the low 62, with less than a 10 percent chance of late afternoon showers."

The next day, the temperature reached 104 degrees for the first time. It poured all afternoon on everybody's picnics. It was freezing by sundown. And weathermen have been at it ever since, talking about the weather and making things worse.

What weathermen don't understand is that weather is a showoff. It likes attention. The more it gets, the more it performs. And like any performer, the weather is constantly trying to outdo itself to impress the audience.

At the dawn of history when people didn't talk about the weather or pay attention to it, the weather thought: "Why bother?" and didn't go to any extra effort. There were no extremes. Then that first weatherman appeared, and there's been hell to pay ever since.

History has shown us that so-called "improvements" in weather reporting have only caused problems. Listed below are a few weather reporting techniques that have been developed throughout civilization, along with the catastrophic weather conditions that followed as a direct result:

Licking a finger and sticking it up in the air – The Great Flood.

Thermometer – The Blizzard of '48.

The Weather Channel – Drought in Africa, earthquakes in Mexico and other devastating recent occurrences that have been unfairly classified as acts of God.

The most disturbing trend in the weather business is the almost gleeful way in which weathermen feel compelled to show us that the weather is worse than we think it is.

It started a few years back when they began reporting the wind chill factor. You would be freezing your buns off thinking it was 32 degrees, which was bad enough. Then the weatherman would tell you it was minus 20 with the wind chill. That would really make you feel miserable.

Have you noticed that since the wind chill factor came into vogue the winters have been getting worse, especially in Florida? I'm telling you, the weather responds to stuff like this.

But what worries me is that weathermen have come up with yet another method of telling us more than we really need to know. It's called the heat index or humiture, and it's supposed to take into consideration the relative humidity when figuring out the temperature.

The other day I was sitting in the living room, trying to survive with just the ceiling fans. The weatherman was on TV. He said it was 97. Then he added: "But with the heat index, the temperature is really 119."

I shut the windows and flipped on the air conditioner. There's an obvious conspiracy between weathermen and power companies.

What's next? Will weathermen start reporting the Torrid Tamale Factor? That's how hot it is if you step into the midday sun having just finished lunch at a Mexican restaurant.

Will they come up with a Swelter Overload Index? That's how hot it is when you get dressed up because the guests are about to arrive, only to have the compressor go out on the air conditioner while you are in the kitchen with the oven at 450 degrees and the kids are pouring grape juice over everything.

I think the only way to get the weather to act the way it used to act is to silence the weathermen. Let them just smile and nod and maybe point to the sky but nothing else. Anyone who gets carried away, especially those who mention things like the heat index, would receive suitable punishment.

Staking them to an asphalt parking lot at noon seems fair. We could all stand around asking: "Hot enough for you?"

Dad Guilt

••••••••••••••

IT WAS MY IDEA TO BUILD THE TREEHOUSE. I admit it. I take full responsibility for everything that happened.

"It will give you something to do with all your free time this summer," I told my sons. "Plus, it will help you develop many useful skills."

Hearing myself say that I realized I sounded suspiciously like a recruiter for the U.S. Navy Reserves. And if the kids had pressed me on it, I knew I couldn't have told them exactly what sort of useful skills they might develop. Because these were skills that I, as a practicing adult, have never managed to accumulate.

But I was serious about the treehouse.

I felt this deep need, this fatherly urge, to toil side-by-side with my sons and build something. Just the three of us. Together. Sweat. Hard work. The joy of seeing our labor transformed into substance.

So, yes, it was more than a treehouse. Much more. It was . . .

It was a bad case of Dad Guilt.

See, I am not a Handy Dad. I am not one of those fathers who, on rainy Saturday afternoons, can take his sons out to the workbench in the garage and there, amid the reversible drills and circular saws and other potentially lethal power tools, magically assemble quaint bird houses or redwood picnic tables.

I have a workbench. Of course I do. Came with the house. Last time I checked, my wife was using it as a laundry table.

The full magnitude of my shortcomings as a Handy Dad began to sink in with my sons when they joined Cub Scouts. Want to hear my theory about Cub Scouts? I figure the Cub Scouts are secretly controlled by the lumber industry. It is a frightening, insidious plot and no telling what sort of obscene profits the big lumber barons are reaping from unwitting Cub Scouts and their dads who are obliged to continually make things out of small blocks of wood.

It starts off innocently enough with the "Pinewood Derby." Cub Scouts must buy an Official Pinewood Derby Kit containing identical blocks of wood. And, from these blocks of wood, they and their dads must fashion miniature race cars.

My sons and I spent many happy evenings at my workbench building their cars. The clean laundry came in handy for absorbing paint spills. And when the night of the big Pinewood Derby arrived we went to the scout meeting anxious to race our sleek, magnificent vehicles.

We were greeted by a heavy infestation of Handy Dads and their sons all sporting wonderfully crafted Porsches, Ferraris and Lamborghinis. They admired our cars and recognized them for what they were: blocks of wood with wheels.

"What kind of cars are those?" asked one smug Cub Scout.

"Classics," I told him. "They are 1947 Hudsons."

But it didn't stop there. No sooner was the humiliation of the Pinewood Derby over than the Space Derby began. We had to buy more blocks of wood and build rocket ships. Let's just say that if there were anything that could make NASA look flawless, then it was our entry in the Space Derby.

Which was followed by the Pinewood Regatta. Boats, this time.

Amazingly, our entries in the Regatta did not sink. But they performed like bathtubs among clipper ships. My sons were discouraged by our complete shut-out in competition where Handy Dads and their sons excelled.

"But have you forgotten?" I asked. "We took first place in the Dad & Lad Cake Bake."

This is true. We really did. I might not be a Handy Dad, but I can cook. And we walked away with top honors in the Annual Dad & Lad Cake Bake when Duncan Hines, my sons and I conspired to make a cake that looked like a hot air balloon.

But my sons were visibly unimpressed by our culinary victory. So . . .

Building the treehouse was to be an act of redemption. It would purge me of Dad Guilt. And it would instill my sons with the confidence that comes from knowing that their old man is not totally inept.

We assembled a vast pile of boards and plywood around a sturdy Japanese plum tree outside my den window. Bo and Dash drew elaborate plans. They envisioned a three-story affair, complete with a penthouse, pulleys and ladders, secret entrances and escape chutes.

The work went quite well. There we were, father and sons, united toward a common goal. I showed them how to work the post-hole digger. The repairman from the telephone company arrived promptly to fix the busted cable. And we really didn't need a sprinkler system in that part of the yard anyway.

We labored on. We sweated. A lot. The boys complained. I reminded them that they were participating in a joyous masculine experience.

"Now hand me that two-by-four," I said.

I should point out that it was, in lumber parlance, a "pressure-treated" two-by-four. I never before understood what that meant. Now I do. It means that if you drop a "pressure-treated" two-by-four on your foot then it will exert a great deal of "pressure" and you will wind up having to be "treated" by a doctor.

The doctor says I have a "non-displaced fracture," which is medical parlance for a cracked bone. If I'm lucky, he says, it won't become terribly arthritic.

My sons, I am pleased to report, did develop a useful skill. From now on they will call a contractor if they want something built.

And me? Well, there is still a big pile of two-by-fours under the Japanese plum tree. I am thinking about sawing them into small blocks. And recouping my losses by selling those blocks of wood to unwitting Cub Scouts.

Any Questions?

AT THE RISK OF appearing uncharacteristically profound, let me just say: Everybody has got to be from someplace.

Deep, huh?

If you'd like to take a few seconds out to ponder the stunning metaphysical ramifications of that statement, go right ahead.

Just don't nod off on me. Try imagining how Olympic orator Jesse Jackson (Silver medal, Mexico City 1968, Uneven Metaphors; Gold Medal, Munich 1972, Freestyle Platitudes) would deliver such a weighty message.

Jesse: EveryBODY!

Crowd: EVery-body! EVery-body!

Jesse: I say, EVVVVVVVVVerybody!

Crowd: EVVVVVVVVVerybody!

Jesse: I say, EVVVVVVVeryBODY has GOT-TO be!

Crowd: Got to BE, Jesse, GOT to be!

Jesse: From someplace.

Crowd: Huh?

So don't think about it too hard. Just accept it. Everybody has got to be from someplace. And, lucky us, we got to be from Florida.

What this means is that, as Floridians, we are accountable for the place we are from.

Whether on the road or in our own tourist-laden back yard we must often encounter People From Someplace Else and be subjected to their stereotypical vision of our state.

"How do you put up with the heat in Florida?" they ask. "What about all the bugs? Is Miami really as bad as they say it is? Don't you get tired of all the tourists? I bet you go to Disney World all the time, don't you?"

It could be worse. Much worse. We could be from Iowa. How do you make conversation with Iowegians anyway?

You: So, uh, how are your pigs?

Or we could be from Nebraska ("How 'bout that corn?") or from Massachusetts ("Ever been hit on by a Kennedy?") or from Arkansas ("Gee, married any first cousins lately?")

But we are Floridians. And, frankly, all the questions that we're asked have become a bit tiresome. We just can't be bothered.

Still, we don't want to appear impolite. Plus, we wouldn't mind impressing People From Someplace Else with our brilliant repartee when they ask us these dumb, stereotypical questions about Florida.

So ... I come to your rescue with: Snappy Comebacks for Floridians.

DUMB, STEREOTYPICAL QUESTION NO. 1: You're from Florida? How can you possibly stand all that heat?

The Philosophical Response: "Heat? Is it really heat or just a lesser degree of cold? And, when all is weighed, am I not a better person for having stood it?"

The Doomsday Response: "Well, we're all gonna burn in hell anyway. At least Floridians have a shot at enduring it."

The In-Your-Face Response: "You have to be in top physical condition, which obviously explains why you live where you do."

DUMB, STEREOTYPICAL QUESTION NO. 2: Florida? Ughh. What about all those awful insects?

The Gourmet Response: "You mean you've never had love bug pate?"

The Friendly Carrier Response: "Oh, some of those little bugs are just precious. And they can give you some of the most exotic diseases. By the way, I am contagious."

The Share-the-Bounty Response: (After reaching into pocket): "Oh, you mean like THESE?"

DUMB, STEREOTYPICAL QUESTION NO. 3: Is Miami really as bad as everyone says it is?

The Totally Objective Response: "Compared to what? Beirut? Baghdad?"

The Crafty Anglo Response: "No hablo ingles."

The Merita Response: "Heck no. Miami's a great place. No problems down there. I got a friend who just moved to Miami. Loves the place. Just loves it. He's got a great job. He's a tail-gunner on a bread truck."

DUMB, STEREOTYPICAL QUESTION NO. 4: Don't you get tired of tourists day in and day out?

The Yummy Entree Response: "Oh no. There are plenty of different sauces that heighten the diversity."

The O-Positive Response: "Of course not. Otherwise the mosquitoes would be unbearable for the rest of us."

The Richard Petty Response: "Naw, we just think of them as tacky speed bumps."

DUMB, STEREOTYPICAL QUESTION NO. 5: Boy, living in Central Florida, I bet you go out to Disney World all the time, don't you?

The If-You're-Thinking-About-Dropping-In-On-Us-Response: "Yes, it's just delightful. And I make it a point to go whenever we have out-of-town guests who will pay our way."

The What-the-Market-Will-Bear Response: "Oh, I try to get out at least four times a year or however often they raise the admission charge, whichever is more."

The If-You-Can't-Say-Something-Nice-Then-Don't-Say-Anything-At-All-Response: "So who do you like in the World Series?"

Sex Ed. Ahead

••••••••••••••••••

(CAUTION TO IMPRESSIONABLE YOUNG readers: This column contains a graphic discussion of what is often referred to as the "birds and the bees." Your parents might disapprove of you reading it. So here's hoping you get to this part before they do.)

Lately it has become obvious that my 10-year-old son and I need to sit down and have a frank, man-to-man discussion about the sort of things a father must at some point have a frank, man-to-man discussion with his son about. Because my 10-year-old son is not likely to absorb this wisdom any other way unless Nintendo comes out with a new game called "Super Spermatozoa Brothers."

Not a bad idea, actually.

From the "Super Spermatozoa Brothers" instruction booklet: "In the cavernous, inscrutable world of Femalia, thousands of eager 'tadpoles' have been launched on their mission to find Princess Ovum. Only one, Lucky, will be the hero who finds the princess."

(In "Super Spermatozoa Brothers II," the more advanced version, Lucky must avoid Princess Ovum at all costs.)

I can sense that my son is ready for the two of us to have our frank, man-to-man discussion because his main topic of conversation recently has been the general ugliness of girls, a leading male hormonal indicator of the change that lies ahead.

"Dad," he asked me the other day, "who do you think will be the ugliest girl in fifth grade next school year?"

"Gee, son, I really haven't given it much thought ... "

"What about Jane?"

"Well, yes, Jane is quite ugly."

"Or Allison?"

"Uh-huh. Allison is ugly, too."

"What about Courtney?"

"Ugly, ugly, ugly."

"I think it will be Jenny. Definitely. Jenny is THE ugliest."

The ugliest girl in my fifth grade was Carol Ann Crenshaw. Carol Ann Crenshaw was so ugly that whenever I passed her at school I was overcome with a chemical urge to go out of my way to slug her in the arm.

I must have been pretty ugly, too. Because Carol Ann Crenshaw would slug me back.

One day we were just standing there, slugging away on each other, when suddenly it was as if I were looking at Carol Ann Crenshaw through somebody else's eyeballs. You know how in artsy films they put gauze over the lens and everything winds up looking all foggy and dreamy and the violins start playing? It was a lot like that.

And I absolutely did not want to slug Carol Ann Crenshaw anymore. Never. Ever. What I wanted to do was . . . was . . . hell, I wasn't quite sure what I wanted to do. That was the problem. It took quite some time before I figured that next part out. Too long, as a matter of fact.

Carol Ann, bless her, took advantage of my stupor to get in several unanswered slugs. And then she was gone. I just stood there watching her, all goofy and jelly-headed. I am pretty sure I heard violins.

And life has never been the same.

So it is important that my son and I hurry up and have this little talk of ours. Even more important now that our public school system has decided to expand its curriculum and offer all students sex education classes.

As you know, this has been quite controversial. I, for one, am strongly opposed to my children learning about sex in school. Oh, they can talk about sex at school all they want. But I want them to learn about it from me, a noted authority, before their teachers even bring up the subject. Because I don't want them to suffer like poor Billy Barwick.

Poor Billy Barwick was this kid in my seventh grade general science class. When I was in public school, seventh grade general science class was where, for one entire week, they instructed us in life's sweet mysteries.

Obviously, this information was so very potent, so overwhelming, that the moment it was revealed there was no telling what might happen. That is why they went to all the trouble of putting the boys and girls in different rooms when they bestowed this knowledge upon them. It was like, if you were even breathing the same air as a member of the opposite sex it could get you in serious trouble.

Hmmm. Come to think of it, that remains, essentially, true.

Anyway, you know how seventh grade boys are. Seventh grade boys already know everything. There is nothing you can tell a seventh grade boy. So most of us already knew everything there was to know about sex. Our parents had sat us down for our little talks. Either that or we had gotten word from older guys. Plus, we had independently devoted long hours to sex research, poring through Webster's dictionary finding dirty words and actively exchanging ragged copies of *Playboy*.

We weren't about to let on that this sex education was news to us. We filed into our boys-only general science class looking bored and all-knowing. None of us bothered to even bring along a pencil and paper. I mean, they weren't going to test us on this stuff.

Our teacher, Mr. Glenn, got right down to business, pointing to a diagram of a naked man and saying: "These are the male gonads. And they manufacture ... "

"Could you please spell gonads?" It was Poor Billy Barwick.

We all turned around and looked. Poor Billy Barwick was actually taking notes. It was too much. Poor Billy Barwick did not have a clue.

"G," began Mr. Glenn. "O-N- ... " And with each letter the laughter grew louder. Until Mr. Glenn reached "S" and we all shouted: "GONADS!!!"

I am told that the girls heard us in the next room. It was a glorious day in the history of sex education in our public schools.

Unfortunately, Poor Billy Barwick was saddled with a highly distasteful nickname for the rest of his high school career. And on graduation day, when Poor Billy Barwick headed up for his diploma, someone on the back row just had to call out: "Give me a 'G!'" We are still remembered as a class of excellent spellers.

So yes, I am going to have that frank, man-to-man discussion with my son as soon as possible. I am looking forward to it.

"Well, son, it's like this," I'll tell him. "There's this tadpole named Lucky and this princess and ... "

He's a Lady

• • • • • • • • • • • • • • • • •

YOU DON'T WANT TO KNOW ABOUT how I recently spent five hours at the Florida Bureau of Motor Vehicles office getting a new driver's license, do you?

I didn't think so. You've been there. You've served your time. In Florida, we all have our war stories from the driver's license front.

So I don't suppose you'd want to know about how I recently spent five hours at the Florida Bureau of Motor Vehicles getting a new driver's license and discovered that I was really a woman, do you?

Oh, really? You mean that has never happened to you at the driver's license office? You have never gone in to renew your license and had the person behind the counter punch some keys on the computer and then look at you and say: "Hmmmm, our records indicate that you are a female."

You don't have any experience with that sort of thing?

Oh well, sure, of course you do.

The driver's license office is always crowded. There is no such thing as a private conversation between you and the person behind the counter at the driver's license office.

"This guy in front of me just found out he is supposed to be a woman," said the man in line behind me.

Florida has become a wonderfully diverse state with people from many different nations and ethnic backgrounds now lining up to get driver's licenses. The information about my gender was soon translated into at least three languages, all the way down the line.

Such situations call for considerable aplomb and dignity, weapons you are supposed to check at the door of the driver's license office. Luckily, I had concealed a small emergency arsenal.

"The sex-change operation was not entirely successful," I told the person behind the counter, speaking in a much-higher-than-usual voice. "But I did get a rather large settlement from the surgeon."

The personnel at driver's license offices take special training in countering attacks of aplomb and dignity. This particular person just stared at me. Then she stared at her computer screen. Then she stared at me again. It seemed as if she were trying to determine if my beard was held on by tiny strings looped over my ears.

Then she uttered the words that no one who already has spent half their afternoon in the driver's license office wants to hear: "I am going to have to call Tallahassee about this."

You want to know how all this got started? Sure you do.

See, I had been driving with an expired driver's license for three years. But it wasn't my fault. Really. It was all a big mistake. Really.

When I changed addresses a few years ago I went straight to the driver's license office, like any good citizen, and reported the change. They issued me a new license. This only took something like two-and-a-half hours.

Like anyone with a new license all I cared about was how good my photograph turned out. I looked pretty good. I had been able to suck in my cheeks and camouflage the double chin.

I did not notice that my birth date was listed wrong, making me a year and six weeks younger than I really am. Nor did I notice that my driver's license I.D. number had changed. What had happened, I learned later, was that the person behind the counter had punched some keys on the computer and confused me with another Robert J. Morris. There are several of us in Florida these days. Of all of us, I like to think that I take the nicest driver's license photograph.

"I am sorry, but I cannot cash your check," a store clerk told me several months after I got the new license. "Your driver's license is expired."

"Impossible," I told her. "I just had it renewed."

Sure enough, she was right. I called the driver's license office. They said I would have to come in, that a matter of this gravity could not be settled over the phone. I told them I could not afford to spend another two-and-a-half hours standing in line. They said I could make an appointment. The first appointment was two months later. I took it. In the meantime I cashed no checks. I drove very carefully.

"Your license is expired," I could just imagine the highway patrolman saying.

"It's not my fault. Really. It's all a big mistake. Really."

"You mind stepping out of your car and walking this white line here?" he would say.

I arrived promptly for my appointment. An hour passed. I didn't make it to the counter. I wasn't even close.

I had things to do. People to see. A life to lead. I left.

Okay, so I let three years go by without getting a new license. Things happen.

I just never got back to the driver's license office. I got used to never cashing checks, except at my bank where they know me. And I continued to drive with extreme care. Maybe everyone should conduct their lives as if their driver's licenses had expired.

Actually, I did return to the driver's license office once, about a year ago. I waited an astonishingly brief 45 minutes to reach the counter, but soon discovered I had forgotten my birth certificate.

When I finally returned this last time it was with great resolve. I cleared out my schedule. I brought along a couple of books to read. I didn't even make a big deal about it being the driver's license office's fault. I took the sign test, the multiple choice test on highway regulations and the road test. Without complaint.

And I waited very patiently during the 20 minutes it took the person behind the counter to talk with Tallahassee. The people behind me seemed considerably less patient.

"Some kind of computer foul-up. We have had to start a brand new file for you," said the woman behind the counter, as if this might wreck the entire state budget. "But we now have you in there with all the correct data. And as a male."

"You mean . . . you mean it's goodbye to my life as a woman?" I asked.

The person behind the counter just stared at me. Then she waved me toward the door.

As I walked away, I heard the guy behind me whistle. It was a wolf whistle. And it was directed at me.

I turned around. I offered him a gesture that, for the benefit of the rest of the line, did not need translation. I curtsied. And I left.

Blue
Memory

MY BROTHER AND I WERE ON A quest: Find the swimming hole we used to visit as teen-agers. And it was obvious that the idyllic place of memory was no longer quite the same when we came to the barbed wire fence. There was a "No Trespassing" sign.

But the gate was unlatched. So I eased it open and my brother and I walked through.

The day was stifling as only Florida can be in the summer, the heat a liquid thing. The deer flies strafed and stung and drew blood.

"Get heat stroke. Get eaten alive. And get arrested for trespassing," said my brother, Skellie. "Yep. That's my idea of a great way to spend a summer afternoon."

A hundred yards down the dirt road we came to another fence, another trespassing sign. This time the gate was locked.

Skellie and I looked at each other, shrugged, then climbed over.

Crossing the second fence we were suddenly in the cool of the swamp. The bay and the cypress were thick, the shade welcome. The swamp was pretty much the way I remembered it – primordial and other-worldly. The interstate highway was not even a half-mile distant, yet the swamp was far removed. And, like any swamp worth calling a swamp, there was the sense of the ominous.

We came to another "No Trespassing" sign. And beyond it a big hand-lettered sign that said: "Keep out." And beyond that a sign that said: "Beware of dog."

"I don't much like the idea of dogs," said Skellie.

"Sign doesn't say dogs," I pointed out. "Says dog."

"Oh, well, sure, in that case . . . "

About that time we spotted the first cage, just off the side of the dirt road. It was bigger than my garage, some 15 feet tall. The food and water dishes were the size of garbage can lids. It looked empty. We walked cautiously past, only to come upon another, bigger cage.

"If those cages are empty then it means whatever dogs were in them are out running around," said Skellie. "And if those dogs need cages the size of those cages then ... "

I didn't see further need to debate him about the dogs. Through the trees we could barely make out a house and a couple of four-wheel drive vehicles. And just beyond, I knew, was the place we used to go for a dip on hot, summer afternoons.

But you just simply do not come walking out of a swamp unannounced and into a situation like that – big dogs and "no trespassing" signs and such.

We decided to turn tail, find out who lived there, call them and ask permission to visit our old swimming hole.

We called it Blue Sink because, whenever water bubbles deep out of the ground in Florida and no other name is attached to the place, then Blue Sink it becomes.

Blue Sink sat in the middle of a swamp just to the west of where they built the interstate. Back in the 1960s, when we used to do our swimming there, a lone gas station was all to be found at the interstate exit. We'd park behind it, then head for the swamp.

Attacking the swamp around Blue Sink was an adventure of large proportion, not to be attempted alone, or even by small numbers. The dirt road didn't exist then and there was no marked trail. You stepped into the swamp and slushed through the muck and the duckweed just knowing a water moccasin was within striking distance. You got lost and doubled back on your path and were black with slime from head to foot, not convinced all the hardship was worth it when suddenly you burst through the vines and the brambles to find ...

It was so blue, a blue I've not seen since. And clear and cold, and if ever I had a glimpse of Eden, then Blue Sink was it. It was maybe 150 feet across and perhaps half that deep. A small stream trickled out, feeding a big lake to the south. Bass and bream and freshwater mullet congregated around the spring boil. The virgin cypress stood sentry like cathedral spires. It was a place wholly and blessedly unto itself.

And such a gift it was in a brutal, unending summer. Leaping in the water was an ice dagger to the heart, but a lift for the soul.

In all the times we ventured to Blue Sink there was never anyone else there. It was a sanctuary we took for granted. It was nature unrefined.

It had been 25 years since last I visited Blue Sink, but not a summer has passed that I hadn't envisioned it.

Turns out that back in the 1970s, a husband and wife bought the 40-some-odd acres surrounding Blue Sink. They built a stilt house right next to the water and a boardwalk clear around the spring's perimeter, something you could never get away with given today's wetlands laws.

And this couple was not inclined to entertain surprise visitors.

We learned this from the couple's son-in-law, who met us at the end of the dirt road. Over the years, the stretch of highway that runs under the interstate had become home to truck stops, gas stations, restaurants and motels.

And Blue Sink was no longer so blue.

"None of the places around here are on sewer and the spring was getting all the run-off. Diesel fuel and used oil mostly," said the son-in-law. "Some of the places dug ditches into the swamp and just dumped straight into it."

He said he'd tried for two years to get authorities to end the dumping.

"But you know how quickly the government works," he said.

Maybe, he said, he could talk his mother-in-law into letting us take a look at the place. He'd get in touch.

And so, I remember Blue Sink the way that it was. Like so much of Florida, it is a place best served by memory.

What's Left?

I WANT TO LIVE AS LONG AS THE next guy. I am willing to do whatever it takes.

I gave up smoking in college. Smoking everything.

I have stopped chewing tobacco. Except for every so often when I do some manly thing like hunt or fish. Then I might take a cheekful of Levy Garrett loose leaf or maybe gnaw on a cigar. But I assure you, I do this only to enhance the male bonding experience. Male bonding is healthy. I read that somewhere.

I don't drink as much as I used to, at least not the hard stuff. And when I drink a tad more than is reasonable, I don't mind taking aspirin. I know it is good for my heart.

I have cut way back on red meat. It is a major occasion anymore when I treat myself to the greasy barbecue I so dearly love. Even more radical – I have actually started taking the skin off my chicken. I eat a lot of fish. So much fish that my stomach rises and falls with the tide. The fish is grilled, not fried. And definitely not slathered with tartar sauce, which contains, pardon me, mayonnaise. One taste of mayo and you go to Healthy Heart Hell.

I drink a lot of coffee. Used to be they thought coffee was terribly unhealthy. All that caffeine. So I cut back some. Then they decided that caffeine was not all that bad. It was the de-caffeinated brew that would do you in. This will probably change yet again. All I can do is adjust accordingly.

I grow vegetables in my back yard. Organic vegetables. I eat lots of them. Raw. It gives me plenty of fiber. Why, some days my gut gets so much fiber that, well, I needn't go into the details. Except to say that fiber certainly does live up to its reputation of keeping one regular. But this, too, is healthy. Very healthy.

The last two cookbooks I bought were: *The Low Cholesterol Gourmet* and *The Gourmet Guide to Low-Sodium, Low-Fat, Low-Cholesterol, Low-Sugar Cooking*. I much prefer *Chef Paul Prudhomme's Louisiana Kitchen*. In fact, at this very moment I would practically kill for a plateful of shrimp etoufee and a slice of sweet potato-pecan pie. But I have come to the sad conclusion that I will not live as long as the next guy if I look like chef Paul Prudhomme.

So I jog. I go for long walks. I play basketball games in my driveway with the neighborhood kids. I go windsurfing whenever I get the chance. I swim laps in the pool. Sometimes I lie down in front of the TV and do sit-ups and push-ups while I watch CNN. I am not an ultra-serious bicyclist, but when I do get out it is for more than just a lazy wheel around the block. Also, I recently bought one of those ridiculous-looking bicycle helmets that makes me look as if I am wearing a mixing bowl on my head. Might help me avoid a concussion if I crash. Healthy.

The last time I visited the doctor's office, a nurse took my blood pressure and said: "Your numbers look excellent." Then the doctor came in and performed a Fiberoptic Zygomodscopy. My editor tells me that good taste (his) prevents me from giving you a thorough rundown on what this involves. All you need to know is that when I scheduled my Fiberoptic Zygomodscopy I did not mark my calendar by writing down "Doctor's Appointment" as a reminder. I wrote down: "Roto-Rooter Exam." The key element in a Fiberoptic Zygomodscopy is a three-foot flexible tube with a teeny, tiny video camera attached to the end. Use your imagination. Anyway, the doctor says my colon looks just swell, thank you. Although next time I have a Fiberoptic Zygomodscopy I am definitely going to ask the doctor for my own personal videotape of the procedure so I can see what that teeny, tiny camera sees. That way I can pop it into my VCR at home and show off just how healthy I am. Or at least that particular three-foot section of me.

Ahem.

I drink a lot of water. This flushes out my system. Immensely healthy.

I used to sneer at the very idea of protecting my skin at the beach. Hey, I am a Florida guy. But now I wear No. 40 sunblock. And a hat.

I do not live near a toxic waste dump or high-voltage power lines or incinerators or a nuclear plant or a factory that spews out stuff that is bad for the air. And if I did I would move.

I drive 55. With a seat belt.

I look both ways before crossing. I watch for falling rocks, yield where I am supposed to yield and am cautious of soft shoulders. I do not exit from the monorail until the exit light appears and the vehicle has come to a complete halt.

Although I do not subscribe to *Longevity* magazine, whenever I go to the newsstand I at least flip through it. I occasionally walk through health food stores. I don't buy very much. But I do breathe deeply. I figure that maybe I will pick up something healthy by osmosis.

So.

How obvious can I make it?

I want to live as long as the next guy. I am willing to do whatever it takes.

Statistics tell me that the next guy is living to be about 72 these days.

Seems like a nice enough age. And I was happily shooting for it until along came Diane Halpern of California State University and Stanley Coren of the University of British Columbia to tell me to hang it up. The next guy, according to the Halpern-Coren research, is a cinch to live 10 years longer than me.

Because I am left-handed.

Left-handers are six times more likely to die of accidents, the research says. And left-handers are more prone to catch certain neurological and immune system maladies that will do us in. Before our time.

"My father is left-handed and in his 80s," one of my colleagues cheerfully mentioned to several of us lefties who were sitting around grousing the day the good news broke.

"So what?" snarled a comrade-in-arm. "He's just taking away some of our statistical years."

Obituaries. I have never paid much attention to them before. But, suddenly, now I am. And it seems to me they could stand to be a tad more complete.

"Joe Schmoe, 67, LH, died today."

That's all I'm asking. Just a simple notation. Just to inform those of us who care about these things.

Otherwise life, as they say, goes on.

I am still left-handed. Like, what am I supposed to do? Switch? Amputate? Grow a small, vestigial arm somewhere on my back so that my dominant arm is actually my middle arm? Even then, it would depend on which way you look at it. There'd be research.

Hell, I might just start smoking.

Smoking everything.

Time Leak

• • • • • • • • • • • • • • • • • •

WE ARE RUNNING OUT OF TIME. THERE IS less and less of it to go around these days.

Theories abound on just what can be done about it. The most popular theory: We are not actually running out of time. We just don't know how to manage the time that we have. Books have been written. Fortunes have been made. Endless seminars have been held – all consuming a great deal of time and contributing to the worldwide shortage of time – in which people instruct other people in how to properly manage time.

The problem here is that time, like certain 8-year-olds, cannot be managed. Time gives the illusion of being orderly, ticking off as it does in neat seconds and minutes and so on. But that is sly camouflage. A trick.

Time is basically subversive. Time cannot be trusted. That is why it is referred to as "Father Time." Not "Mother Time." If time were feminine then the people who yearn to manage time might have a chance. "Mother Time" would run a tight ship. Everything would be operated on the up and up. There would be no time to waste.

But time is masculine. And therefore sloppy. That explains why things have gone all to hell. Father Time was the original anarchist. Father Time sired disorder. And chaos. Father Time is quite the stud.

Time has its pride. It does not beg for money. Rather, time stands on a street corner begging to be wasted. But people who study time management walk by, ignore the plea and chuck quarters at time instead. They cannot buy time. They might as well be studying how to manage other natural phenomena that are utterly beyond control, like lightning or mildew or Don King's hair.

Plus, you cannot be on time. Ever. Being on time is like being on gravity. It is a metaphysical impossibility. Especially since we are running out of time to be on.

So what is happening to all the time? Why, for instance, did you start puttering around in the back yard just a few minutes ago and suddenly it is three hours later and you don't have time to repair the rotten soffit by the front door before it's dark? Or why are you still working on the book you started reading last summer? Or when was the last time you got out to see a movie?

"I used to have so much more time!" you find yourself saying all the time.

It is true. You did. Time has been disappearing. Disappearing in vast gulping quantities. Ever since the beginning of time. There was only a limited amount to start off with. Before too much longer – I would estimate by the year 2067 – there won't be any time left at all. The concept of "running out of time" will have a stark finality to it.

You know what I suspect? I suspect there is a time leak.

You know that big gaping hole in the ozone layer that is letting in all the harmful ultraviolet radiation? That's where the time is leaking out. As a result, all our time is collecting in far-flung corners of the universe. Why, if you were on Alpha Centauri right now you would be positively awash in time. You could start repairing the rotten soffit and, by the time you finished, it would be yesterday.

There is nothing you can do about the time leak. Nothing at all. But it might help you to know that time leaks faster from some places than it does from others.

For instance. Time leaks very slowly from baseball games. Go to a baseball game and, while you don't actually accumulate time, two hours can seem like a week. Especially after they stop selling beer in the seventh inning. Time also leaks very slowly from dentist offices, political debates and your 4-year-old daughter's spring ballet recital.

Time leaks very quickly in places like Wal-Mart. Go into Wal-Mart and, even if you immediately turn around and leave, it is automatically two hours later. And Home Depot? Time is swallowed whole in Home Depot. Especially if you are trying to match fittings for your sprinkler system and wind up with the three-quarter-inch coupler instead of the one-half-inch elbow. And on your way home after your third trip it will occur to you that you still forgot the PVC glue. We're talking two days of time leakage – at the very minimum! – each and every time you set foot in Home Depot.

In addition to the time leak we must also contend with the Time

Suck Continuum. It is growing geometrically. The Time Suck Continuum began thousands of years ago when man created the sundial, a primitive way of trying to bring Father Time under control. The first sundial sucked in only an infintesimal amount of time. Father Time was not particularly concerned. But then the sundial begat the clock which begat the pocketwatch which begat the wristwatch which begat the Swatch. You've seen the TV commercials. You are being advised to change Swatches with the frequency you change underwear. A different Swatch for every day of the week. Each consuming a tiny granule of time. Time is getting sucked up all over the place. Father Time is running scared.

Plus, some countries, like Canada, have begun to hoard time. Go to Canada and you will notice you have lots of extra time on your hands.

"Canada is boring," Americans sometimes say when they visit. "There is nothing to do here."

Which isn't true. Which isn't true at all. There is plenty to do in Canada. It's just that when you get finished doing it all you have lots of time left over. That's because Canadians are stockpiling it. There's even reason to believe they are sneaking across the border at night and stealing some of our time while we are asleep.

That explains why you have been waking up tired lately. Blame it on the Canadians. It is their way of getting back at us for acid rain.

"Why, you can't absolutely prove that," we told the Canadians when they accused us of causing the acid rain that drops on Canada. Then we nudged each other.

Go to Canada. Tell some Canadians you suspect they are stealing our time.

"Why, you can't absolutely prove that," they'll say. Nudge-nudge.

But it's okay because the Canadians will probably sell our time back to us at a fair market price. We'll get a much better deal on time than the Japanese who ran out of time a long time ago and are already living on borrowed time from China. In China the time leaks very slowly. No one wears Swatches.

It's all connected. Someday you'll understand. If there's time.

The Nekkid Truth

Bob Morris is a fourth-generation Floridian and a columnist for *The Orlando Sentinel* and *Florida* magazine. He is a graduate of the University of Florida, holds season tickets for Gator football games and believes in the second coming of Emmitt Smith. Among his most dubious achievements – founding the Queen Kumquat Sashay, held annually in downtown Orlando for people who would not be permitted in any other parade. He has won lots of prestigious journalism awards, but is far too humble to mention them, mainly because they didn't pay meaningful amounts of money. He would include more tasty, biographical details here, but he despises writing in the third person. Besides, you'll learn too much about him just by reading this book. Just keep in mind: He is much thinner than he appears on the cover.